DENI

Smart Homes + Smart Schools = Smart Kids

SCHOLASTIC CANADA LTD.

Scholastic Canada Ltd.
123 Newkirk Road, Richmond Hill, Ontario, Canada L4C 3G5

Scholastic Inc.
555 Broadway, New York, NY 10012, USA

Ashton Scholastic Limited
Private Bag 94407, Greenmount, Auckland, New Zealand

Ashton Scholastic Pty Limited
PO Box 579, Gosford, NSW 2250, Australia

Scholastic Publications Ltd.
Villiers House, Clarendon Avenue, Leamington Spa, Warwickshire
CV32 5PR, UK

Acquisition: Patty Pappas
Editing: Fran Buncombe
Cover Design: Terence Kanhai
Text Design: Derek Chung Tiam Fook
Production: Anna Orodi

Canadian Cataloguing in Publication Data

Overall, Denise
Smart homes + smart schools = smart kids

ISBN 0-590-24772-7

1. Critical thinking in children.
2. Creative thinking in children.
I. Title. II. Title: Smart homes plus smart schools equal smart kids. III. Title: Smart homes and smart schools equal smart kids.

LB1062.093 1997 370.15'2 C97-930943-3

9 8 7 6 5 4 3 2 1 7 8 9/9
Printed and bound in Canada by Webcom Ltd.

For Christian
who quite rightly claims
"If I hadn't been born, she couldn't have written the book,"

and for David

CONTENTS

FOREWORD

I've written *Smart Homes + Smart Schools = Smart Kids* for two audiences: parents and teachers. Surveys indicate that 85% of parents want to take a more active role in their children's education but don't know how; I want to help those parents understand their role. I also want to reach out to those teachers who are trying to make their classroom a more engaging, dynamic place for their students; these "reflective practitioners" are combining the best theory and practice as they design innovative classroom instruction for their students. I hope this book will promote conversation between those parents and teachers as equal partners in supporting their children's intellectual and social development. I hope, too, that it will promote a new respect for the roles and responsibilities of both partners in ensuring school success for every child.

In my current role as curriculum co-ordinator and staff developer in a large metropolitan school district, I give hundreds of workshops for teachers, students and parents. When I present new ideas for promoting better thinking in the classroom, I sometimes hear complaints from teachers that increasingly they are expected to pick up the slack because parents don't take enough interest in meeting their children's needs. They see kids as unmotivated and unwilling to accept academic challenges. They are frustrated when parents don't monitor homework assignments or come for scheduled interviews.

On the other hand, parents often approach me at the end of a presentation excited about the new possibilities for promoting creativity and critical thinking but finding little evidence of what I've described in their own children's classrooms. And when I work with students, especially older adolescents, I find many of them convinced that neither their parents *nor* their teachers are willing to encourage more shared problem-solving and independent decision-making.

Current research indicates that parents *must* be involved in their children's education; no other factor has more impact on a child's success in school. But how teachers and parents can best support each others' efforts needs to be redefined. And frankly, we can't wait much longer. As we approach the 21st century, the need for complex thinking skills is accelerating. Research indicates that if students entering the workforce in the year 2000 don't have a wide range of critical- and creative-thinking skills, their job prospects will be limited. Already our young people are finding it difficult to get established in a career. Employers are more and more selective. They want employees with proven academic and research skills who can also get along well with others, show initiative, leadership and self-management skills, and adapt well to new technologies. And that's just to get a foot in the door!

Helping children to consolidate, personalize and apply their learning is our joint task as parents and teachers. As we look for new ways of teaching and coaching them to think more effectively, we need to share our thoughts. *Smart Homes + Smart Schools = Smart Kids* will, I hope, encourage that process.

CHAPTER 1

HOW ARE WE INTELLIGENT?

A few years ago I was invited to present an evening session for board employees on thinking skills. On the flyer that went out to different departments and schools I called the workshop "How are you intelligent?" Soon after it was distributed, four or five phone calls came back pointing out that there was a mistake on it. Surely it should read "How intelligent are you?"

I started the workshop by addressing this issue. Was I speaking to a group of adults, all gainfully employed in various capacities within our board, who were still wondering if they were smart enough? What measures did they think that I, a relative stranger to most of them, could use to determine how intelligent they were? I'm no psychometrist and certainly wouldn't be administering any I.Q. tests. And even if I did, what difference would a score make at this stage in their intellectual development?

That experience wasn't as unusual as you might think. Very often I find teachers and parents concerned about whether their children are smart enough — smart enough for *what* I'm not sure. I noticed the same preoccupation with measuring intelligence in the adult students I taught. Many were terrified to return to school because, in their minds, that meant once again judging their competency and self-worth by the standards of academic success.

Actually, what I wanted to talk about that evening was a different question, one I find much more intriguing: how is each of us uniquely intelligent?

Three kinds of intelligence

Much has been written over the past ten years about different kinds of intelligence, especially in the work of three American experts: Howard Gardner and David Perkins from Harvard University, and Robert Sternberg from Yale. Gardner's study of multiple intelligences is probably most familiar to teachers, but I have also found Sternberg's model extremely helpful in thinking about students and the many ways they demonstrate their intelligence. I enjoy his research because it's presented in the form of stories about people he's met and students he's taught in the graduate program at Yale. And I find his concept of *practical intelligence* fascinating. It fits my own belief that school should prepare students for something other than more school. If students can't take what they learn in my classroom into other contexts — whether that's their family relationships and friendships, their part-time job, the student council, or their rock group — then I wonder what it is I'm teaching.

I've found that knowing a bit about Sternberg's model is a godsend for many students as well; it makes them realize that, while "school smarts" are important, there are other ways people can be intelligent. They are often surprised to hear that being good in school isn't as much a predictor of later success as they've assumed. Biographies of some of the C.E.O.s in large corporations make it clear that practical intelligence is a much stronger factor in their success than the marks on their transcripts from school.

Some parents feel relieved as well when I describe the profiles of different forms of intelligence. Many can identify in their own children characteristics of intelligence that don't match the profile of academically talented students. Sometimes they've been pretty hard on those kids, haranguing them to be more like an older brother or sister who has excelled in school. Or they've downplayed their children's accomplishments in other areas, because they didn't believe those accomplishments were as valuable as academic achievement.

One example I encountered recently was a high school senior, a dynamic leader in her school and in a provincial student organization. She was helping to organize an international youth conference, but when her math mark slipped, her parents insisted that she give up her position on the organizing committee so she could devote more time to studying. The skills she was using as a student leader (plus the important political connections she was making) were of less significance to them than her score on the latest math test.

Sternberg's *The Triarchic Mind* provides a different perspective on what constitutes learning for various types of smart kids. His initial research was based on a study of his own students, both while they were at Yale and after they had left to pursue careers in a variety of fields. He summarized his theory in the stories of three young women he called Alice, Barbara and Celia. (I'll call their male counterparts Alec, Bob and Carl.)

Academic intelligence

Whenever I share Sternberg's work with teachers or parents, I always start with the Alice brand of intelligence by asking them to describe the student who walks off with all the prizes at the end of the year, the one everyone would characterize as a "good student." What kinds of thinking does he or she demonstrate? Why does he do so well at school? Why do the other kids call her unflattering names?

The list comes quickly:

- good at memorizing and giving back what the teacher says;
- organized, neat;
- punctual, hands assignments in on time;
- doesn't question the teacher;
- does well on tests;
- gets good marks on research essays;
- logical.

(A kid's list will likely includes things like "has no social life" as well!)

Basically, school smarts is an easily recognized and highly rewarded form of intelligence. Sternberg certainly had lots of Alices and Alecs in his classes at Yale, since one of the prerequisites for admission to a graduate program at an Ivy League university is high marks on a standardized examination.

Creative intelligence

However, he also had a very different kind of student, as characterized by a woman named Barbara. Barbara bombed on the Graduate Record Exam and wasn't even being considered by the university's admissions committee. But Sternberg had a chance to review her application and her letters of reference from professors she had had as an undergraduate. They all commended the creativity she had demonstrated in her original research. Being a bit of a Barbara himself, he liked the idea that here was a student who had some fresh ideas to contribute to his field, so he appealed the committee's decision to reject Barbara.

When he was told that Yale's high standards couldn't be compromised, Sternberg hired Barbara as a research assistant, and in the end, when her work lived up to her reviews, the university relented and admitted her to the program. Unfortunately, not all Barbaras are as lucky in having their talents recognized or in finding a champion who will work them in through the back door. There are many Barbaras and Bobs among the hordes of high-school dropouts who can't make it within a system that is still more amenable to Alices.

Practical intelligence

Somewhere in the background — not racking up the top marks or suggesting the most original ideas — was another student named Celia, the one with practical intelligence. She wasn't an obvious candidate for student-most-likely-to-succeed, but when Sternberg did his follow-up research four or five years after graduation, Celia was the one most often moving ahead in the "real world."

Celia is more likely to be in the top ranks of the Fortune 500 companies at some point than either Alice or Barbara is. Plunk her down in the middle of an organization and she'll quickly figure out who the real movers and shakers are and negotiate a mentor relationship with someone who has the expertise she needs to learn. She also picks up on all the unwritten rules and guidelines (the stuff that never makes it into the policies and procedures manuals) that she'll need to know to get ahead. She's got a pretty clear picture of her strengths and weaknesses and knows enough to hire a Barbara and an Alice when she gets a chance to build a team. She's entrepreneurial — willing to take a risk when the time is right. While most of us have fairly fixed ways of dealing with a new situation, Celia is more flexible, adapting when that's appropriate, pushing others toward change when that's a better option, recognizing a no-win situation and cutting her losses.

The Celia type is often simply biding her time in the classroom. The rigidity of roles and the preset curriculum don't leave her much room to negotiate in a traditional school. Co-operative education programs that include job placement are more appealing to students who learn through practical experience. They may also learn more through extra-curricular activities than they do in the regular classroom. If you didn't recognize their talents the first time round, you'll definitely twig to the Celias and Carls when you attend your 25th anniversary class reunion. As you pass their Mercedes in the parking lot, try to avoid an incredulous *"Him? Her?"*

Oh, in case you're wondering what happened to Alice, you'll find her in the staff room or at the front of your son or daughter's classroom. Maybe part of the reason schools still seem most comfortable with the Alice intelligence is that the Alices and Alecs often stayed in school, since that was the context most accepting of their particular brand of intelligence. Teachers are often wary of outsiders who have a vested interest in changing schools, but most don't think of themselves as part of a group with an equally vested interest in preserving the school-smarts brand of intelligence.

Family models

Before we get thinking about our children, I'd like you to spend a few minutes thinking about what kind of intelligence was most valued in your own family. For instance, which of the following behaviours would have been commended, praised or rewarded by members of your family? Circle the number that best corresponds to the following scale:

1 Behaviour actively discouraged
2 Behaviour ignored
3 Behaviour accepted but not singled out for comment
4 Behaviour commented upon favourably
5 Behaviour singled out for positive comment or reward

1.	Paying attention to detail	1 2 3 4 5
2.	Memorizing and reciting facts	1 2 3 4 5
3.	Organizing information neatly	1 2 3 4 5
4.	Taking things apart and putting them back together correctly	1 2 3 4 5
5.	Meeting deadlines or finishing work quickly	1 2 3 4 5
6.	Getting high marks on tests, examinations	1 2 3 4 5
7.	Following directions exactly	1 2 3 4 5

8.	Telling jokes, making up riddles	1 2 3 4 5
9.	Retelling or acting out stories	1 2 3 4 5
10.	Creating original works of art	1 2 3 4 5
11.	Disassembling objects and putting them back together in new ways	1 2 3 4 5
12.	Playing with an imaginary friend	1 2 3 4 5
13.	Collecting odds and ends	1 2 3 4 5
14.	Singing, dancing, clowning	1 2 3 4 5
15.	Keeping a diary or scrapbook	1 2 3 4 5

16.	Selling lemonade or setting up other small businesses	1 2 3 4 5
17.	Negotiating a better deal on allowance	1 2 3 4 5
18.	Sharing a hobby with an older child or adult	1 2 3 4 5
19.	Peacemaking among kids in a dispute	1 2 3 4 5
20.	Exploring, going off on adventures	1 2 3 4 5
21.	Being elected to a leadership position in a youth organization	1 2 3 4 5
22.	Trading, bartering toys	1 2 3 4 5
23.	Doing a Tom Sawyer and getting others to help out with chores	1 2 3 4 5

Now let's advance the clock a few years. Which of these behaviours are typical of you as an adult?

1 Not interested
2 Could be fun but doesn't suit my personality
3 On my list of things to try
4 Something I do on occasion
5 Like Tigger, it's what I do best!

1.	Working on projects that require attention to fine details	1 2 3 4 5
2.	Playing games like Jeopardy that emphasize quick recall	1 2 3 4 5
3.	Reorganizing home or work space for maximum efficiency/neatness	1 2 3 4 5
4.	Assembling objects by following instructions systematically	1 2 3 4 5
5.	Establishing goals and meeting deadlines	1 2 3 4 5
6.	Taking courses (and continuing to get good marks!)	1 2 3 4 5
7.	Building a reputation as a model employee	1 2 3 4 5

8.	Entertaining others with jokes, stories	1 2 3 4 5
9.	Playing computer simulation games	1 2 3 4 5
10.	Juggling several projects or hobbies	1 2 3 4 5
11.	Inventing new ways of doing things	1 2 3 4 5
12.	Daydreaming	1 2 3 4 5
13.	Filling basement/garage with stuff that will come in handy soon	1 2 3 4 5
14.	Singing, dancing, writing, playing a musical instrument	1 2 3 4 5
15.	Keeping a journal	1 2 3 4 5

16.	Setting up a business	1 2 3 4 5
17.	Negotiating deals on small- and large-ticket items for home	1 2 3 4 5
18.	Discussing decisions with a mentor	1 2 3 4 5
19.	Acting as a mediator in home or work disputes	1 2 3 4 5
20.	Changing jobs several times	1 2 3 4 5
21.	Providing leadership at work or in a community organization	1 2 3 4 5
22.	Playing the stock market, gambling	1 2 3 4 5
23.	Still conning friends into helping out with home repairs	1 2 3 4 5

See any patterns? Very often the intelligent behaviours that we value as adults have as their source what we experienced as models of intelligence in our formative years. What our parents and teachers chose to notice or ignore, praise or condemn, reward or punish helped us to establish our own definition of intelligence. That five-year-old's mind map that we took with us on our first day of school is still a compelling guide to our adult explorations of the world of the intellect.

And it's a powerful influence in our interactions with children. Let's play with that idea a bit.

Defining intelligence

What model of intelligence might you unconsciously (or maybe quite consciously) be promoting to your own children? Think back to the last opportunity you had to provide a child with feedback about what constitutes intelligent behaviour. What was the behaviour? Was your feedback positive, negative or neutral? (Use the 1-5 scale we looked at for our own childhood experiences, or recall what form the feedback took. If it began with "How many times do I have to tell you," it was probably low on the scale!)

Are the behaviours you respond to positively similar to or different from those that were rewarded in your childhood family? If you think in terms of a Venn diagram, where would your map and your child's map of intelligence overlap? Where would they differ? Perhaps you'd end up with something like the sample in Figure 1.

Figure 1

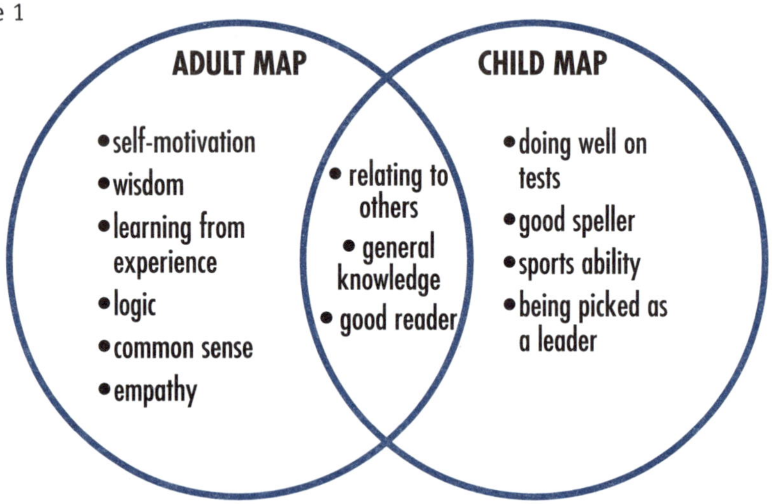

In one of our frequent car conversations, I tried this discussion on with my 11-year-old son. Knowing and being able to talk about science was at the top of his list of intelligent behaviours, especially astronomy and chemistry. Analyzing was important to him. His list included a few surprises as well, like being able to use big words that others don't recognize. He readily agreed with my belief that a person can be intelligent in many ways, and gave the example of a girl in his class who was struggling academically but was really good at drawing. On the other hand, much of my list of intelligent behaviours (creativity, humour, curiosity, being interested in lots of different topics, making new connections) had no particular relevance for him.

Research studies clearly show differences in what kids and adults value as intelligent behaviour — although, interestingly, 10-year-olds typically value school performance and general knowledge, with a particular emphasis on reading and mathematics. Kids and adults both value getting along well with others, but kids also put a high premium on sports ability as a sign of being smart. Only adults mention motivation, showing interest in peers, and creativity.

In *Competence Considered*, Sternberg suggests that these overlapping but significantly different maps of intelligence may lead to miscommunication between children and adults. What the school-age child values as intelligent may not carry much weight with Mom and Dad, and certainly some of the behaviours that we as parents would love to see in our offspring, like the ability to function independently and responsibly, are nowhere in their picture!

From the world of work

If the academic research of Sternberg, Gardner and others isn't reason enough to rethink how schools and parents respond to the needs of differently intelligent children, then recently published reports from the world of work might be convincing. Already in the 1980s, particular skills were being identified as highly desirable for employees entering the work force by the year 2000. The examples I'll use here are from an Ontario government report, but similar studies can be found across the country and in other areas of the world. While acknowledging that education has many goals other than preparing students for future employment, those reports are nevertheless fairly consistent in recommending that schools should be paying attention to the demands of the workplace when designing instructional opportunities for all students.

Essential skills

The Ontario *Generic Skills/Economic Development* report highlights competencies in three specific areas as essential for success in the work force.

As Figure 2 on the next page shows, most jobs in a rapidly changing, information-based workplace require the ability to:

- manage information through the application of critical and creative thinking strategies;
- get along well with others in complex social interactions;
- respond to technological changes confidently.

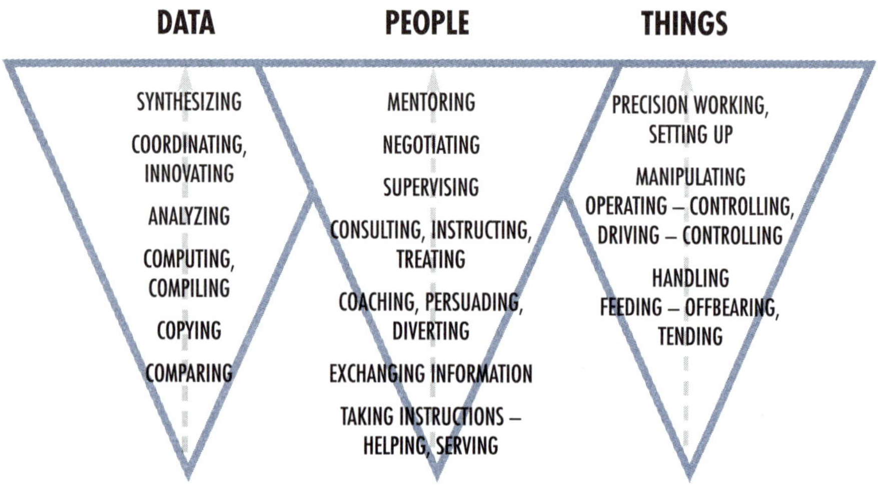

Figure 2 **The skills on the upper end of each scale are those the report finds in short supply among the labour force.**

Many adults in the existing workforce are experiencing difficulty in meeting the demands of the workplace because they lack either formal education or on-the-job training. As new communications technology like the Internet makes more information immediately accessible to anyone with a PC and a modem, the ability to synthesize large amounts of data and to sort out the wheat from the chaff becomes a more highly valued thinking skill. And creativity is a bonus, since it's the company that can find an innovative use for this information that has the potential advantage over a competitor.

When we look at the social side of the picture, we find that many employees now work outside traditional hierarchies in work teams where roles and responsibilities are shared. These new structures require more sophisticated interpersonal skills. It doesn't take much social savvy to follow direct orders; it's a lot more complicated to constantly negotiate working relationships with co-workers. With lifelong learning the order of the day, employees often benefit from establishing strong coaching or mentoring relationships that meet the needs of both parties. As middle-management positions continue to disappear, front-line workers need to demonstrate initiative and self-management abilities and a willingness to solve problems and make decisions independently.

In outlining what work requires of schools, the SCANS 2000 report from the United States reinforces the broad-based competencies that workers of the future will need. In addition to outlining the basic literacy, numeracy and information management skills, the report specifies the kinds of thinking skills that are the foundation for life-long learning:

Thinking Skills:	Thinks creatively, makes decisions, solves problems, visualizes, knows how to learn and reasons

A. Creative Thinking	generates new ideas
B. Decision Making	specifies goals and constraints, generates alternatives, considers risks, evaluates and chooses best alternative
C. Problem Solving	recognizes problems, devises and implements plan of action
D. Seeing Things in the Mind's Eye	organizes, processes symbols, pictures, graphs, objects and other information
E. Knowing How to Learn	uses efficient learning techniques to acquire and apply new knowledge and skills
F. Reasoning	discovers a rule or principle underlying the relationship between two or more objects and applies it in solving a problem

Employees who are flexible and willing to learn continue to be attractive to employers. On the other hand, the prospect for workers who do not demonstrate these "habits of mind" is grim. Job redundancy will most likely be their lot. Worse still, they may not be candidates for retraining if their skill levels in the three areas diagrammed in Figure 2 are perceived as substandard.

Balance is the key

Looking at these reports from the perspective of Sternberg's triarchic model, I see employers suggesting clearly that they are not looking to hire an Alice, a Barbara *or* a Celia. What they want instead is Dynamic Debbie or Diversity Dave, a super-worker with a balance of all three kinds of intelligence. There's definitely a place for Alec's academic research and information-management skills, but with a liberal dose of Bob's ingenuity and enthusiasm for innovation. Add Carl's entrepreneurship and people skills to the mix and we're talking valued employee.

If, like me, you're troubled by all the recent articles about 20-somethings who can't get a first job or 30-somethings who are returning to the nest (with spouse and a couple of kids in tow), you may find this research compelling — and a strong motivator for re-examining your own notions of what intelligence looks like in the 90s. Maybe even what school should look like. Where's the textbook that teaches ingenuity? Can you learn teamwork skills by burning the midnight oil?

Several years ago I was asked to do a presentation for parents of students in a gifted program at a local secondary school. Teachers in the school were finding increasing resistance from parents to student participation in extra-curricular activities and field trips. Any teaching strategy that wasn't classroom or textbook based — in other words, that wouldn't serve as the basis for a question on the final exam — was considered a waste of the students' time.

Instead of making a speech, I asked the parents to form small groups and share with one another what they had done in the course of their working day. I asked them to think specifically about the skills they had relied on to complete their workplace assignments. Many of them were professionals with responsible, high-paying positions — a doctor, a lawyer, a pharmacist, a teacher, a research engineer — and when they had sorted and classified their lists of skills, we could quickly see how their jobs involved balanced competency in the three areas of data management, interpersonal relations and creative use of technology.

My question back to them was how they thought their children would learn these skills, which they had identified as essential to their own success. If their children's teachers were to focus instruction in one or two areas exclusively, what supplementary opportunities were they, as parents, prepared to provide to ensure a more balanced profile? What kind of portfolio would their sons and daughters be able to provide to an employer, or a faculty admissions panel, that would indicate they were preferential candidates for highly competitive positions? Dirty trick using parental ambition to make a point? If a pragmatic look at our kids' future helps us to avoid limiting their present options, I'll risk it.

Changes in the classroom

Slowly schools are beginning to broaden the spectrum of intelligences they acknowledge. The idea that there may be alternative ways children can process and demonstrate their understanding of academic concepts is starting to gain credence. A few schools have even taken the extraordinary step of restructuring their classrooms, their timetables and their assessments to bring instructional practices more in line with theories of multiple intelligence. However, parental understanding and support are essential if these innovations are to be more than localized experiments.

The following chapters present in more detail some of the approaches that provide opportunities for school and home to work in partnership to support children's intellectual development in its many facets.

SUMMARY

People define intelligence and demonstrate their own intelligence in different ways. Usually our adult perception of intelligence is based on what our parents and teachers chose to praise or condemn when we were young. Because today's workplace requires people to demonstrate multiple intelligences, we may need to re-examine how our schools are teaching thinking skills.

CHAPTER 2

WHAT ROLE DO PARENTS AND TEACHERS PLAY?

In his book *The Unschooled Mind,* Howard Gardner suggests that schools could learn a lot about teaching from children's museums. So, on a recent trip to Boston I went to the ever-popular Boston Children's Museum to see what lessons were there to be learned. The opportunity to stand back and observe parents and children interacting with the museum's displays was an eye-opener.

Who teaches? Who learns?

It first hit me in the bubble room. Here was an exhibit that couldn't be simpler — large vats of soap, glycerine and water and a variety of objects, from string to metal, that could be used to make bubbles of different sizes and shapes. The challenge was to make bigger, longer-lasting, more elaborate bubbles by experimenting at the different stations in the room.

But again and again I saw the same phenomenon: parents grabbing the objects and shouldering the children aside so they could make the bubbles while the kids looked on. Invariably the parents provided a running commentary, telling the children what they should be observing and learning, but they didn't let the kids create their own bubbles and make their own observations. Dads seemed to be particularly quick at jumping in to direct the activity and turn bubble-making into Chemistry 101.

It struck me what a valuable opportunity those parents were missing. If they had stood back and observed their children at the various displays, what insights they could have gleaned. Perhaps they would have seen new dimensions of their children's learning and cognitive styles. Often, because we are so engrossed in our usual adult/child scripts in which we provide the teaching and the kids produce the learning, we lose the power of unique moments like these.

Another great display in the museum focused on the human body's many fluids. Kids could see a whole bathtub, and one cut in half, approximating the amount of blood in an adult body; nearby was a tiny vial representing the amount of tears shed in an average crying jag. They could stretch out a tape-measure over six metres long — the length of the small intestine — or check out the realistically full toilet for the amount of waste matter excreted each day. The kids couldn't believe what they saw when they lifted the lid on the toilet! They rushed off to drag other kids over to share their discovery that nothing had been left out of this wonderful display. Thank goodness there are adults who are still mindful of a five-year-old's curiosity and wonder, and who make a learning tool of children's fascination with bodily functions and all its taboos.

I couldn't help thinking about how, as parents and teachers, we could provide similarly rich, meaningful experiences for our children, experiences that allow for "the having of wonderful ideas." Step one is probably the most difficult: back off to give children the time, space and initiative to organize their own encounters with the world around them. As David Perkins observes in his book *Smart Schools*, getting teachers to let go of the executive functions so that children can share responsibility for both the learning and the teaching that go on in the classroom is one of the most difficult and most critical steps in creating smarter schools.

When working with parents and teachers I often ask three questions I first heard posed by Sternberg:

- Who planned the child's day? (what to wear, what to eat, what learning activities to complete, what books to read, what home work to do, what time to go to bed)
- Who monitored the events of the day, making necessary adjustments to deal with the unexpected? (a sudden change in the weather, a forgotten lunch, a last-minute assignment, a can-celled practice, a missed ride home from the mall)
- Who assessed the day's activities and provided feedback on accomplishments? (administered a test, gave a compliment, handed out the rewards or punishments, declared the day a winner or prayed for a better tomorrow, put failures and disappointments into perspective)

Teachers are often quick to point out that these are the jobs that validate their picking up a paycheque every couple of weeks; parents lay claim to the same functions as evidence of their commitment to the well-being and success of their children. So I ask them all to ponder the implications of Sternberg's follow-up comment that the people doing these three jobs — planning, monitoring and assessing — are the ones who are going to bed smarter each night! We've all seen newspaper pictures of children who get to be town mayor or fire chief for a day, but how comfortable are we with the idea that children need *daily* opportunities to "administer" if we want them to acquire the higher-order thinking skills that characterize highly effective adults?

A lesson in humility

I am reminded of my experience in trying to teach my son how to tie his shoes. Typically, I was the one who decided the magic moment had arrived when he should learn this skill, although he had expressed no real interest in doing so. I decided to use the standard demonstration model: I would tie my own shoes, slowly explaining each step while he watched, then he would try while I provided coaching and feedback, and we would keep at it until he mastered the task. Within minutes we were locked in a battle of wills, and very little actual shoe-tying was happening. I was threatening a return to velcro; he was going barefoot for life.

A week later I looked down and his sneakers were tied. Impossible. I hadn't finished the lesson. Questioning revealed that there was a lacing board at his preschool. Seems the kids could mosey over there and practise tying and untying to their heart's content, without adult interference. There were also dolls and a Sammy the Snake, whose sections were joined with buttons and zippers and other kinds of fasteners, including laces. All fun to play with. I've since learned, too, that there are shoe-tying songs and poems about bunnies hiding behind trees and jumping down bunny holes that are a lot more entertaining than my lecture on shoe-tying.

One of the benefits for both teachers and parents when we back off from our sage-on-the-stage role is that we are free to observe what children actually do when they want to learn something new, and to consider a wider variety of options in our teaching methods and learning materials.

A child's view of learning

A more respectful approach might also address a major roadblock to learning for many children: a skewed concept of what it means to learn, which many kids develop at a fairly young age. In his book The *Unschooled Mind*, Gardner describes the typical child's view of learning this way:

> "You go to school, a smart person tells you something, and you are expected to learn it and remember it, and if you don't you are stupid. Rarely is there any conception of learning as a long process of experimentation, reflection, and self-improvement; rather learning depends upon having certain abilities, or more broadly, having a good mind. Especially in the scholastic milieu, one's merit as a self is closely allied with assessment of how good your mind is." (p.94)

I would guess that for many children, especially those whose parents have taken to heart the maxim that a parent is the child's first teacher, that concept of the adult as expert and arbiter of the child's success as a learner is firmly in place before school comes along to reinforce the message. But think of the new freedom for children if we could change that mindset and persuade children that:

- learning is not just the domain of the classroom;
- everyone starts off as a beginner when learning something new, even adults;
- nobody is good at everything;
- the struggle is the learning.

These are messages that children need to hear and see from us if we want to assure them that they aren't stupid.

A new view of teaching

As a classroom teacher I frequently experience crises of confidence. They occur most typically when I'm eavesdropping on student conversations following a weekend. When I worked with adult learners, many of the stories I heard were about problems that provided perfect opportunities for applying all the wonderful problem-solving and creative-thinking skills we'd been learning in the classroom. Yet I heard little evidence that all my hard work in teaching active listening and negotiation skills, or in generating alternative solutions, even crossed their minds when they were actually trying to work through a problem.

And I don't think I'm alone in this. How many of our former math teachers would want to be held accountable for what we do in filing our income tax returns? Or science teachers to hear our answers to questions like "Why is the sky blue?" How would we do in a county fair spelling bee? Would our shop teachers really care to check out the maintenance records on our family vehicle? As parents, do we ever shudder when we read editorials in the paper recommending legislation holding parents responsible for their children's actions? As teachers, when we think about it, have we ever really taught any kid anything? I was in the middle of one of those bouts of soul-searching when a friend told me a story that got me back in the game with a whole different understanding of what it means to teach.

Brian, vice-principal of my school and a former phys ed teacher, shared with me his reading about a research study done in the United States to figure out what makes a winning football team. Instead of taking the usual approach and analyzing the players, the researchers decided to focus on the coaches. They identified winning and losing coaches and followed them around, observing what they did.

The study found a key difference in the two groups. Winning coaches would introduce a new play to their team and, on average, have them practise it 999 times before using it in an actual game. When they finally did transfer to a game setting, the play was repeated at least 20 times per game. On the other hand, when losing coaches introduced new plays, they allowed only five or six practices. If the players hadn't got it by then, the coach would scrap the play and suggest a different one instead. The players never had a chance to perfect any new play; in fact, they got more and more incompetent with each successive short-lived play.

Brian assured me that this wasn't a story about the relative intelligence of college football players, but a realistic description of the learning process. Typically, we teachers underestimate the amount of practice kids need to achieve mastery of complex skills, particularly thinking skills. Nor do we provide the skilled coaching that solidifies the practice, because we can't wait to get on to the next lesson. The end result for the kids is the same as playing on or rooting for a losing team: frustration. If, instead, we were to figure out what "plays" we really want to teach to support our students' cognitive development, and give them the amount of time they need to make those plays part of their repertoire, we might actually see some results.

Intellectual coaching

I keep coming back to Brian's story. Let's say that as a teacher I value independent critical thinking and want my students to be able to detect bias in all its forms. How can I provide them the 999 rehearsals they need? Probably I can't if I see myself as working alone in my classroom. But if I start thinking about the other contexts the kids also operate in — if I add in the amount of time they spend watching television, for example, and arguing with friends and reading advertisements — that number of rehearsal opportunities starts to look like a snap!

I expect a winning coach doesn't see himself as the whole show either. He's got assistant coaches and talented players who can take responsibility for reinforcing his instruction. He's probably got videotapes of the key plays, so his team can see what those plays look like when they're done right. He can use his players' other experiences as well, showing them how this play is similar to or different from something they've already mastered. As the players develop confidence, they may find their own ways to modify and improve the basic plays to suit the team even better, or start inventing plays for themselves. In game debriefings, they can talk about how they're adapting their coach's instruction.

But for this kind of rich learning to happen, we all have to start on the same page of the same game book. Then we can figure out together how to get that practice going.

Defining the learning target

There's a wonderful chapter in Stephen Covey's best-selling *The 7 Habits of Highly Effective People* that I frequently re-read. The story he tells of turning over responsibility for maintaining the front yard to his eight-year-old son is essential reading for any parent interested in enhancing a child's intellectual and social development. It demonstrates the increasing evidence coming from the field of assessment that most learners can hit a learning target if two conditions are met: first, the target must be clear; second, it must hold steady.

In coaching his son, Covey took the time first to establish clearly what a model front yard looks like (fortunately, the next door neighbour's yard provided the needed contrast), and then to define the target they were aiming for. "Clean and green" became their rallying cry. He brought the model even closer to home by using the garden hose to bisect the yard and working with his son to clean one half first. Then they stood back to compare the two sides.

Covey isn't describing this as a thinking-skills lesson; he's talking about how to get kids more involved in taking responsibility. But the modelling he's providing for his son is the essence of cognitive coaching. Taking the time to debrief an activity is what solidifies and consolidates the learning. An important aspect of that discussion is evaluating why things were done in a particular way, how modifications to the steps or sequence might change the results, what was enjoyable or difficult about the process, how we might approach it differently another time. That talk has the potential for taking even the most mundane chore out of the realm of boring routine and investing it with significance for learning.

Covey highlights the point where most of the potential for true learning is lost. Characteristically, although parents are willing to share most of the responsibility for a task with their children, they reserve to themselves the privilege of evaluating the quality of the work. Same in the classroom. Ultimately it's still the teacher who assigns the mark. It's the teacher's comment or happy-face sticker that puts the final seal of approval on a job well done.

And yet, the only way to guarantee that a person consistently produces excellent work is to ensure that, as a learner, he or she has internalized the standards of quality that characterize exemplary performance. In other words, the worker must become the ultimate evaluator of his or her own work. In the case of Covey's son, that meant that he took his dad on a tour of the front yard when he was satisfied that "clean and green" had been achieved. And his explanation of how he had achieved these results was as important as the immaculate front yard.

Supporting thinking processes

As adults, we often forget what it was like when we first set about learning a complex new skill, whether that was washing the supper dishes or writing a book report. Because many of the thinking processes that underlie the successful completion of these tasks have become automatic for us, we don't stop to think about the cognitive skills embedded in them. We assume that children know the steps for complex mental processes that may be represented linguistically by very simple words.

For example, teachers often ask primary children to "sort" or "group" objects. But when I ask groups of teachers to define the difference between sorting and grouping, I usually don't get a quick response. Instead, they generate a number of specific examples (sorting laundry, getting the garbage ready for pick up, forming co-operative groups in the classroom, organizing collections, etc.) before someone ventures an explanation of the different steps in the two processes: sorting involves looking at differences among objects; grouping requires looking for common attributes. How children go about making distinctions like this changes over time and with practice. The point is that at times we aren't clear ourselves about what it is we're asking kids to do. No wonder they don't always "get it."

Making thinking visible

One of the growing trends in the classroom teaching of thinking skills is the use of graphic organizers that help address the need to be explicit about the kinds of thinking we anticipate the students will use and the steps inherent in those thinking processes. One of my favourite examples is an organizer used for helping young students make thoughtful predictions about what might happen in a story they are reading.

James Howe's *Bunnicula* series is very popular with kids. The novels feature two main characters, a cat and a dog, and their nemesis, a newly acquired rabbit who may or may not be a vampire (hence the name Bunnicula). One teacher had read the first few chapters to the class and was following up the reading with a typical prediction activity, asking the students to anticipate how the dog and cat might react to the idea that the bunny was a vampire. But this teacher decided to structure the children's thinking by providing them with a graphic organizer.

Deciding which organizer to select required her to do some real thinking about how we go about predicting the possible responses of two individuals to a similar event. As adults we understand the concept of multiple perspectives. We've all had the experience of being present at a meeting or sharing in a conversation and then hearing it reported on later by someone else and wondering if we were on the same planet. But kids often struggle with that concept, and with the idea that previous experience colours our perception of current reality.

The teacher finally decided to use the compare-and-contrast chart shown in Figure 3 (next page) as an organizer.

First, each student completed the top section, listing several ways in which the dog and cat were alike. Then they used the bottom section to explain the differences. The key to this part of the process is the central column, which asks the students to be explicit about the attributes they are selecting for comparison. That leads to step three in the process: looking over the comparisons and deciding which differences are really significant ones that merit further explanation.

The student whose chart I saw shared in the follow-up reading workshop had determined that the most important difference between the two animal characters was the fact that Harold the dog ate books while Chester the cat read them. Because Chester was a devotee of the family's collection of horror stories, he had previous experience (at least second-hand) of what to expect when a vampire arrived on the scene. The student predicted quite accurately that the cat would be more nervous about having the bunny in the house and would be looking for ways to warn the family.

A lot of the fun in reading Howe's novels with a class comes from the children's delight in seeing their expectations realized. By helping her students to make both accurate and meaningful predictions, this teacher was not only enhancing their ability to focus their reading on significant features of the story, like characterization, but also introducing them to thinking processes that will serve them well in many contexts beyond the classroom. In selecting a particular graphic organizer, she was also explicitly sharing her thinking about thinking. That's another way that adults can coach children.

COMPARE AND CONTRAST DIAGRAM

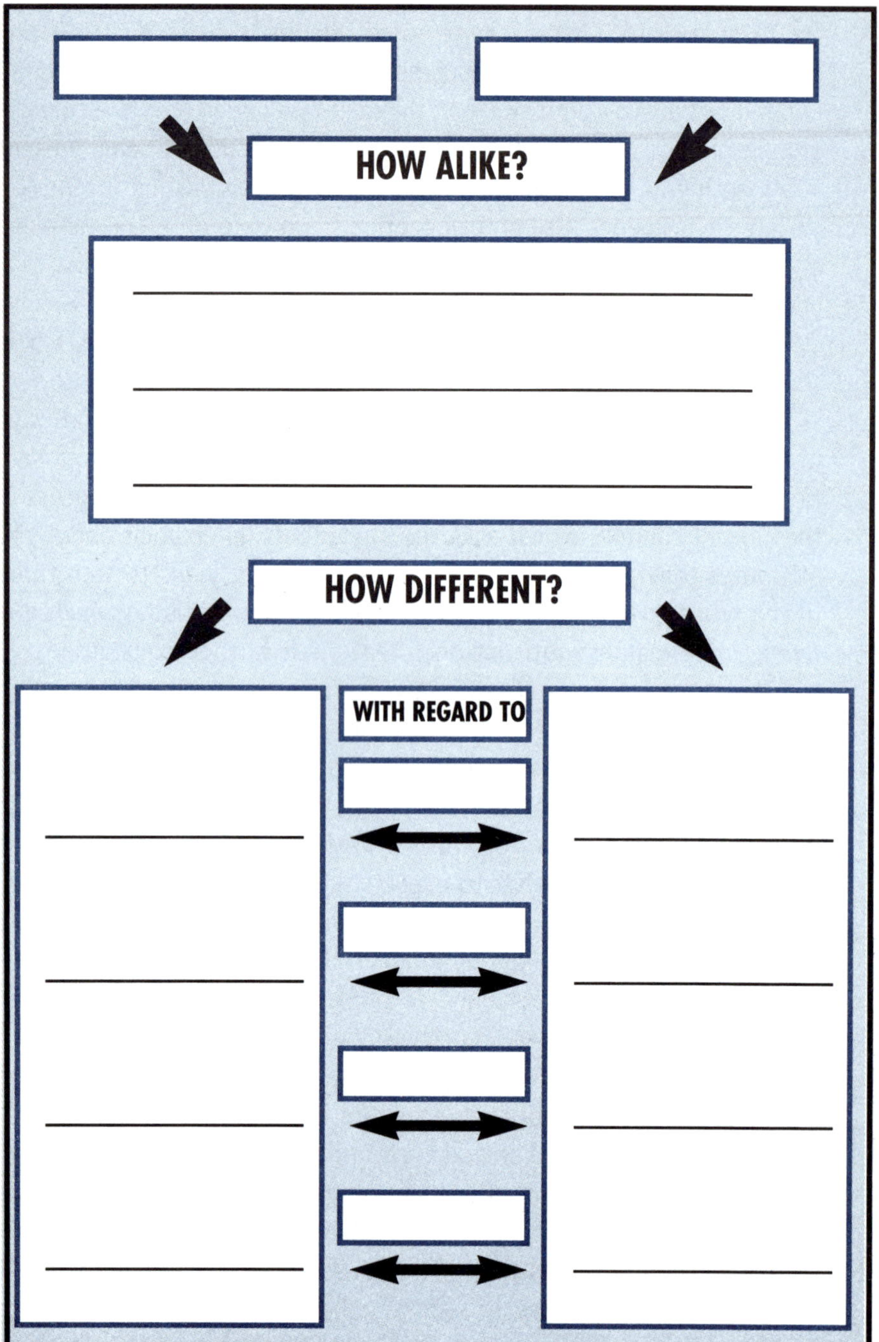

(From *Organizing Thinking* - Book 1, p.11)

Adult models

When we watch young children at work or play, we notice that they usually provide an ongoing commentary on their actions. As they get older, they internalize this "self talk" and probably shake their heads at people who mumble their way through a task or still move their lips while reading. It's interesting that when we adults are confronted by a particularly thorny problem we vocalize our thoughts as a way of keeping track of what we're doing, or of going back over what we've done to find out where we made a mistake. Because most of this dialogue is silent, however, children don't get many natural opportunities to hear us think about our thinking.

We're also more likely to share finished products with kids, after we've worked out all the bugs. They usually don't get to see the lopsided birthday cake before we fix it up with additional icing and strategically placed candles. Because they get the assembled toy, they miss all the cursing at unreadable instructions and the last-minute trip to the store for the batteries the box clearly says are not included. Coaching means being willing to share failure as well as success.

The stupid-smart continuum

Are you wondering how you're doing as a coach for kids' thinking? One of the ways to get some feedback might be to look at behaviours you typically see from the children you interact with. Where kids place themselves on the smart-stupid continuum probably says a lot about what we are doing to support them. Children who feel competent as learners share some characteristics, as do kids who are convinced they are incompetent. Where would you put your children on each line?

trusts own ideas ___________ doesn't trust own ideas
initiates activities __________ waits for others to initiate activities
enjoys challenges __________ avoids challenges
participates actively ________ watches or withdraws
explores new situations _____ avoids new situations
praises self _______________ makes negative self-comments
takes pride in own work _____ doesn't value own work
adjusts quickly to change ____ resists changes to routine

persists with problems __________ gives up easily
handles teasing/criticism well ___ cries when teased or criticized

While some variations in behaviour are to be expected when we take into account differences in learning and cognitive styles, nevertheless we should see children moving toward the left side of the continuum if, as adults, we engage with them in effective coaching.

SUMMARY

As teachers and parents, we must allow children to be responsible for their own learning. However, we can contribute to their cognitive development with the kind of coaching that supports them not only in defining their learning goals but also in evaluating their own performance. With effective coaching strategies, we can help children feel competent as learners.

CHAPTER 3

BEYOND BACKWARD BASEBALL CAPS

Did your kids go through the hat stage? You know, when every new activity had to be accompanied by the appropriate headgear. I still visit with nostalgia the collection of hats my son accumulated around age four. There's a real sailor's hat we bought for him at an antique store, a cowboy hat, a Roman gladiator's helmet and breastplate, a moose hat with antlers, a pith helmet for tropical explorations, a trucker's cap and a surgeon's skullcap. Most of them no longer leave their home in the basement, but six of his collection still get lots of action:

- a white set of bunny ears he got one Easter;
- a red firefighter's helmet;
- a yellow beanie with a propeller on top;
- a black pirate's hat, complete with skull and crossbones;
- a green cap that opens up like a crocodile's mouth;
- a blue Viking helmet that's great for Wagnerian opera.

Why these hats? They're the ones that correspond to Edward De Bono's "six thinking hats." I always use them when I'm asked to talk with teachers, students or parents about different ways of thinking. For De Bono, each colour corresponds to a different kind of thinking:

White hat	FACTS	seeking information, perceiving, objective;
Red hat	WOW	paying attention to feelings, intuitive;
Yellow hat	YES	optimistic, finding potential benefits;
Black hat	NO	identifying problems or errors;
Green hat	NEW	speculating, generating alternatives, brainstorming;
Blue hat	THINK	organizing, planning, monitoring.

Each of De Bono's thinking styles has its time and place, so having all six hats as part of one's thinking headgear is a definite advantage. However, without careful planning, all six hats may not make it into a child's classroom. Like my son's extensive hat collection, some may be relegated to the basement or the locker, leaving some kids hatless.

I love using De Bono's hats with young children. When I ask them to help me identify a student in the class who is particularly skilled in the kind of thinking the various hats represent, they catch on quickly. For example, I ask:

- Who asks a lot of questions? (white)
- Who knows when you're feeling upset or angry? (red)
- Who can turn around the no-good, terrible, horrible day? (yellow)
- Who notices mistakes on the blackboard? (black)
- Who's got the wackiest ideas? (green)
- Who likes to tell us what to do next? (blue)

The hats also work well as a way of bridging cultures, I've found. A group of visiting Japanese educators was curious about how our schools were teaching thinking skills. When I displayed the hats to them, they could quickly identify members of their delegation who exemplified the six different kinds of thinking. We could then talk more easily about which hats would be most valued in Japanese and Canadian classrooms.

Hats in the classroom

De Bono's hats have many uses in the contemporary classroom. Children can be introduced to each hat in turn and practise using that kind of thinking in a variety of different ways. For example, green-hat thinking can be used to generate ideas before writing a story, to suggest alternative solutions to a problem, to build vocabulary. Wearing the green hat, we might ask: How many words can we think of that have the prefix "com"? Then, when we switch to the blue hat and compare the words on our list, we might ask: What do we think the prefix "com" might mean?

The children can also think about when wearing a particular hat might be inappropriate. For example, in an emergency, choosing the green hat might cause you to delay because you're busy thinking about what you *could* do, instead of doing it. Sometimes, too, it's important to use the hats in a particular sequence. If you jump to thinking about solutions for a problem with your green hat before you've used your white hat to gather information, you might find out at the end that you've been trying to solve the wrong problem.

When I work with adults, it's almost always apparent that they find green-hat thinking very difficult; adults aren't as spontaneous as children are in suggesting ideas that might appear ridiculous. Our green hat allows us to put aside our tendency to censor ideas that are impractical or illogical and generate as many possibilities as we can. Then it's appropriate to use our black hat to evaluate those options critically to find one that's practical in the given circumstances. De Bono says he finds the average five-year-old 90% more creative than the average 40-year-old. In part, that's because young kids are so comfortable with green-hat thinking.

Observing students using each hat, teachers can identify the areas of thinking where they are most skilled and those that need extra practice. The hats also come in handy when you want to give feedback about someone's thinking without being judgmental. There's a whole different tone when, instead of asking "Which side of the bed did you get up on this morning?" or saying "Boy, are you negative!," you simply suggest that the person might be using a black-hat perspective. The listener has the option of agreeing with your perception or correcting you: "As a matter of fact, it's my red hat you're seeing. I had an argument with my daughter before I left home this morning and I'm still feeling upset." Or "No, actually I'm wearing my white hat. I'm not asking you all these questions because I dislike your idea. I'm just trying to get a better understanding of your thinking."

When students use the whole set of six hats to explore different sides to a problem, they can experience how different perspectives influence what they see and hear and feel.

Hats at home

Unfortunately, that's a lesson I've been known to forget when it most matters — when working through a problem at home. As a parent, I could frequently save myself a lot of grief if I stopped to consider what hat my son might be wearing at the moment, before reacting to something he's said. That second's pause could save me from replaying an all too familiar script. Here's an example of a quick response that didn't go well.

The scene:	Saturday morning. Time to get ready for dancing class.
The background:	My son has been dancing since he was three years old — ballet, then tap and now jazz. He didn't last too long in the ballet class once it started to get serious. As a matter of fact, the ballet teacher removed him from the class, claiming he was the only child who had defeated her in a 40-year career. My young Fred Astaire's dancing career was in jeopardy there for a while, but fortunately a male teacher was willing to give him a second chance. Indeed, a few weeks previously he had said he was pleased by the effort Christian was putting into jazz classes and suggested that he try a slightly more advanced class. Mom was proud that her son wasn't a total write-off.

The dialogue:

Mom	Christian, it's time to get ready for your jazz class. (Blue hat, organizing the kid as usual.)
Christian	I think I want to go back to my old class instead of the new one I'm in.
Mom	(Immediately grabs for the black hat.) There you go. The teacher gives you an opportunity to prove yourself and you want to quit as soon as the going gets a bit tough. Sure it's easier to go back to the other class, but what's the teacher going to think? You know, Christian, in real life you don't always get a second chance. You've got to put out a little effort or the opportunity might not be there again... (Blah-blah-blah, you can fill in the rest.)
Christian	(Borrows the black hat.) Why are you always criticizing me? Are you saying I'm lazy? Then maybe I should just quit the stupid jazz class altogether.
Mom	(Snatches the hat back.) Right! After all the money I've

spent giving you lessons, not to mention the hours I've sat in the waiting room while you were in there dancing, and the money for the costumes and the fact that we can never get away on a weekend.

Christian — That's it. I'm not going.

Sound familiar? Wrong hat at the wrong time. While he cooled his heels in his bedroom, I wandered into the kitchen where I thought for the umpteenth time how much easier it is to teach thinking skills than to use them with members of one's own family. I ate a piece of humble pie and decided to try it again.

Mom	I'm sorry, Christian. I didn't give you a chance to explain. (Puts on the white hat and goes data hunting.) Why are you thinking that you would prefer to go back to your original class?
Christian	(Starts to cry. Oh! oh! red hat.) I would be so humiliated. Last year the teacher moved kids ahead too fast and then, when they couldn't do the number for the showcase, he put them back and they had to learn a whole new routine at the last minute.
Mom	(Responds to the red hat.) I'm sorry. I didn't realize you were worried about that. What would help you right now? (Invites him to select an appropriate hat.)
Christian	(Selects the yellow hat and finds a positive way to address his worry.) I guess we could talk to the teacher and tell him what I'm thinking. Then we can decide together which class is best for me.
Mom	(Blue hat.) That sounds like a good idea. Shall I speak to the teacher when we go in and ask if he has a few minutes between classes?
Christian	Sure.
Mom	Great, then I guess we're ready to go.

(P.S.: The teacher agreed that Christian was probably better placed in the original class but complimented him again on his enthusiasm and told him how much he appreciated the fact that he had settled down and was willing to give his best effort. Mom resolved to take her own advice and try to adjust her hat more quickly next time.)

We shouldn't dwell on scenes like this that we've all played out many times, but it's helpful to remember how hard it is to change old habits of thinking, even when we know better. Having access to metaphors for different ways of thinking, like De Bono's hats, is useful in those situations when we really do want to try a different approach that might lead to a better outcome for everyone.

Hats at report card time

I find the hats come in especially handy at a potentially volatile time, the arrival of the report card. Why is it that report card time is so stressful for everyone? I recently attended a Monday evening in-service with a group of 50 teachers. The workshop leaders showed us five faces with different expressions ranging from down at the mouth to upbeat. When they asked us to rate our mood that evening, at least half the group was at the lower end of the scale. Why? They had spent the weekend preparing the marks and comments the kids would receive on their final report cards.

When my son arrived home with his report, it looked for an instant as if there wouldn't be many smiling faces at our end either. However, once again De Bono's hats came to mind. I read and responded to the comments very differently when I focused attention on which hats seemed to be honoured in his classroom.

Positive comments that value certain hats

I'm interested to see the classroom behaviours teachers choose to comment on positively, and to consider what these descriptions suggest about the value they place on certain kinds of thinking. I often suggest to teachers that they look over their last set of report cards and categorize their comments using the six hats, and to parents that they review their children's collected reports to see if there are obvious patterns in the comments. For example, the six hats might be reflected in positive comments like these:

Blue hat: organized, punctual, follows instructions, completes all assignments, self-disciplined, accurate, methodical, conscientious, uses time wisely, works independently;

Red hat: caring, insightful, shows empathy, sensitive, thoughtful, responsive to music/poetry/nature, respects others, helps others in class;

Yellow hat: co-operative, sunny, a pleasure to teach, an asset to the class, positive, enthusiastic, interested, perseveres, volunteers, shows initiative, confident, shows pride in work;

Black hat: critical thinker, precise, has good judgment, careful, logical, defends own ideas, questions or challenges opinions;

White hat: masters information, has broad-based knowledge, attends to detail, curious, good research skills, reads widely, participates in discussion;

Green hat: creative, original, has lots of ideas, dramatic, artistic, experiments, humorous, playful, open-minded.

Negative comments that value certain hats

Equally revealing are the behaviours teachers comment on as unsatisfactory or needing improvement. These also suggest the hats students must wear in order to be successful in the context of that classroom:

Blue hat: disorganized, late, rushes work, doesn't complete all assignments, messy, doesn't follow instructions, lacks self-discipline, makes frequent errors in written work, irresponsible;

Red hat: doesn't pay attention to needs/rights of others, withdrawn, doesn't accept constructive criticism, has difficulty expressing feelings;

Yellow hat: unco-operative, easily discouraged, gives up, frustrated, lacks enthusiasm, unconfident, self-deprecating, doesn't show pride in work, moody, has a negative attitude;

Black hat: unquestioning, easily led, impulsive, only sees one side to an issue, fuzzy thinking, uncritical, over-generalizes, illogical;

White hat: lacks general knowledge, needs to read more, doesn't participate in discussions, doesn't ask questions, lacks curiosity, written work lacks detail;

Green hat: lacks spontaneity, has few original ideas, doesn't respond well to changes in routine, work lacks flair/imagination, intolerant of other opinions.

Comments that devalue certain hats

Some remarks can also suggest that the teacher doesn't place a high value on certain types of thinking. What is seen as an asset in one classroom might generate a less positive response in another:

Blue hat: inflexible, has high need for structure/routine, overly concerned with accuracy, avoids risk-taking, bossy, uncertain, constantly seeking clarification;

Red hat: emotional, moody, has difficulty accepting constructive criticism, would do better in class if spent less time socializing with peers;

Yellow hat: overly enthusiastic, lacks critical judgment, dependent on approval from others, too trusting, easily manipulated by others;

Black hat: judgmental, challenges authority, intolerant, has a negative attitude;

White hat: asks irrelevant questions, bogs down in detail, goes off topic, has difficulty persisting with a given task;

Green hat: acts silly, gives inappropriate responses to questions, daydreams, doodles when should be listening, doesn't follow instructions, easily distracted, plays when should be working, continually starts new projects before others have been completed, messy, disorganized.

Different grades, different hats

It's important to note also that, according to research, teachers at different grade levels tend to reward different thinking competencies. Elementary school teachers tend to emphasize social development, so we see more comments about blue-, yellow- and red-hat thinking. These teachers usually see following instructions and class routines, co-operating and getting along well with others as positive characteristics.

As students enter secondary school, however, teachers typically place higher value on verbal reasoning skills, and college-level instructors place the highest value on problem-solving ability. Thus, black-hat critical thinking and white-hat research skills become more important as children progress through the grades. Nevertheless, a more balanced approach to both instruction and assessment, one that values all six hats across all grade levels, might lead more students to feel both competent and successful.

Avoiding comparisons

During a recent education week, I was invited to address a group of parents who had come to a classroom open house. Their grade two children had prepared displays of their work for the visit. The room was filled with notebooks and folders, group projects, spelling and math tests, paintings and crafts. I could see the parents beginning to eye the displays, looking for their own kids' work while sizing up the rest.

I'd already had a chance to look at many of the displays before the parents arrived and knew that the quality of work was varied, as one would expect. There were a few dynamite projects that showed artistic talent. Some of the written work looked better because those students had mastered printing. There were writing folders that were carefully labelled and organized and others that had dog-eared pages hanging out. Even the kids' desks told a story, despite a last-minute cleanup directed by the teacher. The temptation to make comparisons was strong.

I did a quick intro to De Bono's hats and had the parents think about their own repertoire of thinking skills. What did they most value? Which hats did they associate with their children? Were their children in danger of abandoning any of those hats? Had any of them reached the same point as my son, who was quickly limiting his hat collection to one, a backwards baseball cap decidedly black in colour? Did they see benefits in helping to keep their children open to different ways of thinking?

Then I turned them loose on the classroom, but with the suggestion to focus on their own children's work as an archive of the different kinds of thinking the child was using in the classroom. They were to wear their white hats and gather data, which they could then share in a non-judgmental way with their sons and daughters. The white hat invites description, not evaluation. I suggested that they might also want to try a little yellow-hat enthusiasm, sharing their excitement about the potential revealed in their children's work, and some red-hat empathy for the children's delight or frustration with their achievements.

Isn't that a more thoughtful approach to giving children feedback about their accomplishments, whether it's a report card coming home several times a year, a test or project handed in, a musical or dramatic performance, or a chore completed? De Bono's hats remind us to keep our focus where it belongs — on the uniqueness of each child's thinking.

Hats at work

A friend of mine told me that a few years ago a large municipal insurance company trained all of its employees to use De Bono's six hats. They went even further in introducing this new thinking model to their corporation: they painted six hats over every light switch and installed carpet-tile hats outside each elevator so people would see them every time they turned on a light or left their floor. They even renamed the boardroom the Thinking Room.

Does that get your green hat spinning with some new ideas for a little home and school redecorating à la Edward De Bono? Maybe it's time to revisit that old hat collection and try on some ways of thinking that make childhood days such a delight.

SUMMARY

Representing Edward De Bono's six thinking styles with six different colour hats can help us recognize the kinds of thinking we look for in our children. If we wear an appropriate hat for each different situation, and teach the children to do the same, we will reduce the likelihood of family and classroom friction. It's important for all of us to be open to different ways of thinking.

CHAPTER 4

HONOURING EACH CHILD'S APPROACH TO LEARNING

The battle was epic. On one side: the class, made up almost exclusively of 14-year-old boys who had definitely determined that French had no place in their lives. On the other side: me, a teacher invested by the provincial government with the sacred mandate of ensuring that they acquired at least one high school credit in French in order to earn a secondary diploma. By November it was by no means clear whether there would be survivors on either side.

With many years of successful teaching under my belt, I was having real difficulty understanding my inability to get through to this gang. It took all my confidence and strength of will to keep trying to engage them in the exercises prescribed by the text we were following. Each week had its prerequisite spelling tests and dictations. There were nightly homework assignments designed to consolidate the grammar points the lesson was based on. There were a few opportunities to role-play scenes or to act out dialogue, but most of the activities were paper-and-pencil with a heavy emphasis on memorization. It helped if you were an aural learner.

For weeks the boys complained about their inability to remember all these lists of words. Whenever they turned their hands to composition, any grammar points or verb endings we had drilled were long gone. Marking homework and tests was red-pen time, correcting the same errors again and again. Some of the students had trouble just sitting in their chairs for the 70-minute class. You've never heard such creative excuses for getting up and moving around. Every pencil in the joint was sharpened to a nubbin. The runs on the drinking fountain and washroom made my classroom look like the last stop on the local subway line. I was the only one who couldn't seem to work time out of the classroom into the daily schedule. Obviously this was not working.

Fortunately for all of us, I was also teaching a class of adults who were part of a re-entry program in the school. As I listened to their stories of how dropping out of school had severely limited their options in careers and contributed to social and family problems, I kept thinking about my guys down the hall. If I didn't want them to go the same route, what could I do to reduce the growing sense of frustration and failure that wasn't doing any of us much good?

Right-brain/left-brain preferences

Unexpectedly, an opportunity presented itself for me to attend a professional development session given by the famous Dunn and Dunn husband-and-wife team, who had done extensive research on the role of learning styles in academic success. In that half-day session I got just a taste of this exciting new field, but I came back with four key questions that would give me a quick way of looking at right-brain/left-brain learning preferences. I couldn't wait to try them out.

When you are studying or concentrating on learning something new, do you prefer:

A	B
1. total quiet, no distractions	1. background noise, music
2. a desk and chair	2. lounging informally
3. bright overhead light	3. muted or natural light
4. breaks to eat, drink, smoke	4. munching while working

Those who respond with mostly A answers tend to be more left-brained, the Bs more right-brained. Since this research was first popularized, a lot more study has gone into the whole question of brain orientation and its impact on learning. Today, most theorists see it as a useful metaphor, not a literal description of complex brain functioning. Nevertheless, the basic tenet that people have significant differences in the ways they orient themselves for learning still holds.

When I asked my adolescent charges which list best described them, they were almost 100% into list B. That's why they hated the classroom — the fluorescent lights were distracting, the desks were uncomfortable, they were supposed to be quiet and listen, and they got in trouble if they wanted to chew gum or eat candy. Like most right-brained learners, they preferred to focus on the "big picture." All the finicky little grammar points they were required to learn were of no interest to them. Many were strongly visual in their learning. That's probably why they thought they were wasting their time with me; they'd rather be in art class or in one of the technical shops. They preferred to learn by doing; they liked classes where they made things and had something to show for their efforts.

So now what? Since there was no question that the current situation wasn't meeting any of our needs, I obviously had to rethink my approach, and the new information I had acquired about learning styles gave me the push I needed.

I reorganized the classroom so the students frequently worked with partners or in small groups. I also got them out of the classroom entirely for a time, by developing a unit in which they each researched and designed a children's book in French. We had a daycare centre in the school, so they used the preschoolers to check out their early drafts and then actually published their books and donated them to the centre. Several of them turned out to be quite talented in their artwork, and we hung some of their original drawings around the school.

They also worked in small groups to produce slide-tape presentations on Quebec City, which they had visited the preceding year. They even added music to their presentations, featuring French Canadian rock groups. In the library, they researched other countries where French is spoken as a first or second language and designed a travel brochure for prospective tourists.

They still had to do some of the other stuff. There were end-of-term examinations to prepare for, and they continued to lose marks if they goofed up their verb tenses. But they were actually acquiring some French in spite of themselves. And I was getting a whole new training on modifying curriculum and instructional strategies to match student learning styles.

Can they listen to music and do homework?

Educators have responded with different levels of enthusiasm to the Dunn approach to learning styles because of its focus on environmental factors and their impact on learning. Teachers may feel that there are limitations to the modifications they can effect in a regular classroom — although, if they decide that this is an important consideration, they may be surprised at how easy it is to differentiate areas of the classroom and make it more comfortable for more of the students.

For parents, it may be quite easy to use the Dunns' research to create a place for homework that will really meet an individual child's needs. It may also end a lot of unproductive arguing about how kids need to organize themselves for study. Maybe kids shouldn't lose so many of those arguments about studying on the floor or listening to music while reading. In fact, some children probably do find it easier to concentrate when they have background music and can flop. Sitting up straight may not be the moral issue so many of us have made it in the past.

So here's a real opportunity for parent-child collaboration, experimenting with different settings and other elements to find an environment that works. Some of the factors to consider include:

- environmental — sounds, lighting levels, room temperature and furniture arrangement;
- self-direction — high or low need for external structure, level of personal responsibility;
- social — working alone or with a partner, a group of peers or an adult mentor;
- physical — best times for study, need for movement, snacks.

Please don't make the common mistake of assuming that children in the same family have the same needs or preferences when it comes to organizing their study. One child might like to work at the kitchen table while you're preparing dinner; another might need the quiet of his or her own room in order to concentrate. One child may love having you ask review questions; another may prefer to check in periodically with a classmate while completing an assignment. One child may prefer to get homework out of the way before dinner so the rest of the evening is free; another may need a TV or sports break after school and prefer to leave homework for later. You may even have an early-bird who will set the alarm for 6:00 a.m. and do his or her best work in the hour before everyone else is up.

That kids have to do homework can be a house rule. *How* they do it can be open for negotiation. It's really important that kids find a routine that works for them, so daily homework doesn't become drudgery or an ongoing battle. Like adults, children are more motivated to do their best work when they have some measure of control over their working conditions.

The 4Mat model

As useful as the Dunns' introduction to learning styles was, the model that was most helpful to me in the classroom was developed by Bernice McCarthy. I've used it with everyone — students, teachers and parents — because while it encourages us all to accept our own learning styles as valid, it also helps us to recognize that there are equally valid ways of learning that may be directly opposite to ours.

When I worked with a group of parents recently, I had them sort themselves into four groups according to the approach they would take if they were in the market for a new car. Think about which of these options would most appeal to you:

Option 1 — I tell the salesperson a lot about my needs and wishes to make sure I get a car that's perfect for me. If that means waiting a few weeks to get the style, colour and options I want, that's fine. It also helps to close the deal if I like the salesperson's manner.

Option 2 — By the time I get to the dealer, I'm pretty clear about what I want because I've researched my choices using magazines or consumers' guides. I have a lot of questions that I want answers to, however, and expect salespeople to be well informed about the vehicles they are selling. I'm interested in all the fine print about warranties and service.

Option 3 — The test drive is all-important to me. I want to get the car on the road and see how it handles. A demonstrator would be fine as long as it's been properly maintained. I'll be taking care of routine maintenance myself, so I don't need a fancy servicing package.

Option 4 — I'm driving by the dealership and decide to pop in just to check out the new models. If something catches my eye on the lot, I may be in the mood for a little wheeling and dealing. I prefer something with a bit of flash to it, something that makes a statement about me.

The parents quickly sorted themselves into four groups. They were delighted to meet their new partners, since they seemed to have quite a bit in common. Each group, of course, was equally convinced that their method of buying a new car would work best. People in groups 1 and 3 tended to see each other as totally out to lunch, as did those in groups 2 and 4. Here are some of their comments:

Type 2 Imagine just taking something off the lot instead of making sure you get all the options you want! Or even looking at cars before you've done any background research! You've got to be nuts making an impulsive decision on a big-ticket item like a new car.

Type 4 Hey, I've got a friend who practically called Ralph Nader personally the last time she was looking for a car and she still got stuck with a lemon that almost blew up in her driveway when the engine refused to shut off!

Type 1 No, you're both wrong. It's the dealership that matters. Find one you can trust and go back there. You've got to build a relationship through return business if you want the best in price and service.

Type 3 Build a relationship? We're talking about buying a car, not choosing a mate for life. That's why I think used cars are probably the best bet.

Each style has its merits. No one way will work for everyone. That's McCarthy's point when it comes to learning as well. Her "style inventory" helps to identify the factors that make learning either appealing or painful for individual learners. When I ask either children or adults to think about their most and least enjoyable learning experiences, the groups are quick to agree on some common factors:

	Enjoyable	Painful
Type 1	shared learning	controlling instructor
	inviting atmosphere	no opportunity to interact
	personal relevance	read the manual and do it

Type 2	clear instructions textbook to read sequencing units	disorganized instructor role-playing favouritism
Type 3	hands-on practice access to resources coaching when needed	forced group work broken equipment just sit and watch
Type 4	creative instructor open-ended assignments performances	unvarying routine my way or the highway timed tests/examinations

There are lots more ways in which the different types of learners vary, but I think you get the idea. McCarthy's inventory helps people to identify not only their strongest style but also their unique profile. No one is totally a Type 2, for example. I may find that I tend to do best in a classroom that has clear directions, lectures and demonstrations from an expert, homework assignments from a textbook that help me to prepare for examinations — all basic Type 2 strategies — and yet still enjoy group discussions. Another Type 2 may prefer a field trip to a lab and find group discussions a waste of time.

Teaching for all learning styles

The fact that all four learning styles are found in every classroom presents some challenges for teachers when it comes to delivering curriculum. In the past, schools tended to favour Type 2. Students who did well in highly structured environments — where multiple choice tests and essays were the preferred forms of evaluation, and where the teacher's chief role was to present information — typically experienced success. The classroom was a comfortable place for them because the way it operated fit well with their learning style.

However, children who more typically chose the other styles often found the classroom hostile to their way of learning. I think again of all those kids whose report cards imply that there's something wrong with their way of trying to shape the classroom experience to feel more comfortable.

> *Sara would do much better if she spent less time socializing when she is supposed to be working on independent assignments.*

Perhaps Type 1 Sara was talking about the assignment — generating ideas or confirming her understanding by interacting with her peers.

Jovan needs to wait to hear the complete instructions before beginning his task. He is often halfway through the exercise before the teacher is finished explaining.

How typically Type 3 of Jovan. Type 3s are the trial-and-error group who often like to jump right in and muddle about, leaving consulting the manual until they run into a problem.

If Carlos would spend less time daydreaming and doodling, he would stay focused on the topic being discussed.

Ah, but those Type 4s do wander off to other lands and times. Something the teacher said may have prompted a whole series of personal associations and Carlos is thinking about those while the class is on to the next point.

McCarthy's suggestion is for teachers to design lessons and units with the four distinct learning styles clearly in mind — her "4Mat" model. Typically a lesson would include:

- An introductory activity that calls up prior knowledge of, or experience with, the topic to be studied. This engages the Type 1 learner who needs an answer to the questions "Why should I know this? What will it mean to me?" The introduction can also provide an opportunity for discussion with a partner or with the whole class as students share their experiences.
- A carefully structured presentation of the new information, which can take many forms — a lecture, a video, a reading assignment with focusing questions, a demonstration. The Type 2s have been waiting for this part, since they thrive on learning something new.
- An opportunity to practise or apply the new information with monitoring, coaching and remediation, if needed, to consolidate understanding of the concepts presented. The Type 3s are happy because now they are getting hands-on experience, whether that's doing a chemistry experiment or building something in the shop or doing the math questions up on the blackboard.

- An opportunity to take the new knowledge, skills or values and make them one's own. Here's the place for creative projects, either individual or small-group. Type 4s may be happy to choose from a list of selected topics or projects, or may want to do some negotiating. Multiple intelligences, as defined by Gardner's model, are acknowledged when the option to use drama, music, dance, art, creative writing, community service projects or public demonstrations are included as ways of demonstrating mastery of the unit's content.

Not every lesson or unit needs to lead to a huge project or presentation; each of the four steps can be incorporated into even a brief lesson. But if teachers habitually leave out one or more of the steps in the plan, they disenfranchise a group of students by not giving them a chance to shine.

Moreover, the 4Mat process encourages students to stretch beyond their natural style and develop flexibility by acquiring some of the competencies that characterize holders of the other styles. As adults, we know that we often find ourselves in situations that require that flexibility. You may be a great Type 2 researcher, but if you can't summon up a creative spark when it's time to present your idea to the boss, you're not going to have the support you need for your ideas. If you're a Type 3 task-oriented manager with a number of Type 1s on your team, you may have to build some discussion time or even a social component into your meetings if you don't want to be seen as the office Scrooge. On the other hand, if you hire only people who seem to be really easygoing, you may find that, while your department is conflict free, it somehow never seems to meet the deadlines for production. Even the Type 4 "artiste" needs to pay the hydro bill or find himself or herself literally working in the dark!

Kids might as well learn how to strike a balance between doing things the easy, fun way and simply figuring out what the job requires and doing it. The 4Mat approach is a good way to give them the practice they'll need.

The True Colors® approach

If all this talk of different styles sounds interesting but a little too advanced for the young learners in your life, there's an even easier way to introduce the concept of learning styles.

An educator from California named Don Lowry developed the True Colors® program, which describes personality types by using the work of Isabel Myers and Catherine Briggs, a mother/daughter team. The complete Myers-Briggs inventory is widely accepted in business, but Lowry found that using only four basic colours to describe the most significant differences among the styles was more practical for a school setting. His approach simplifies the identification of personal styles by having individuals "try on" the different colour combinations as they interact with others to complete a series of tasks.

When I present an introductory workshop for students, those activities include:

- rank ordering, for themselves, the four cards that describe the different colours (see Figure 4);
- discussing their colour profile with other members of a small group;
- working with others who share their predominant style to plan and present a poster or skit that "brightens" their colour for other class members;
- writing a brief reflection that describes how they might use the True Colors® idea in their interactions with friends or family members.

In a follow-up session, we explore how the different colours might cause conflict among people, and role-play ways of negotiating resolutions to problems while respecting different needs and communication styles.

When I present the same workshop to teachers, it's amazing to see how like the students they are in their approach to the learning tasks. I love to watch, for instance, when we provide the participants with bins of materials, colour-coded to the four styles, for use in developing their presentations. Whether we're working with kids or adults, the results are very much the same:

- The group with a lot of orange in their individual personalities invariably makes the biggest mess as they dive into the boxes and drag out everything to use in their skit. They are often so

I need to feel unique and authentic
◆ **Enthusiastic, Sympathetic, Personal** ◆
I look for meaning and significance in life
◆ **Warm, Communicative Compassionate** ◆
I need to contribute, to encourage, and to care
◆ **Idealistic, Spiritual, Sincere** ◆
I value integrity and unity in relationships
◆ **Peaceful, Flexible, Imaginative** ◆
I am a natural romantic, a poet, a nurturer

◆ **AT WORK,** I have a strong desire to influence others so they may lead more significant lives. I often work in the arts, communications, education, and the helping professions. I am adept at motivating and interacting with others.

◆ **IN LOVE,** I seek harmonious relationships. I am a true romantic and believe in perfect love that lasts forever. I bring drama, warmth, and empathy to all relationships. I enjoy the symbols of romance such as flowers, candlelight, and music and cherish the small gestures of love.

◆ **IN CHILDHOOD,** I was extremely imaginative and found it difficult to fit into the structure of school life. I reacted with great sensitivity to discordance or rejection and sought recognition. I responded to encouragement rather than to competition.

9100

YOUR CHARACTER

I act on a moment's notice ◆
◆ **Witty, Charming, Spontaneous** ◆
I consider life as a game, here and now
◆ **Impulsive, Generous, Impactful** ◆
I need fun, variety, stimulation,
and excitement
◆ **Optimistic, Eager, Bold** ◆
I value skill, resourcefulness, and courage
◆ **Physical, Immediate, Fraternal** ◆
I am a natural trouble-shooter,
a performer, a competitor

◆ **AT WORK,** I am bored and restless with jobs that are routine and structured and satisfied in careers that allow me independence and freedom, while utilizing my physical coordination and my love of tools. I view any kind of tool as an extension of self. I am a natural performer.

◆ **IN LOVE,** I seek a relationship with shared activities and interests. With my mate, I like to explore new ways to energize the relationship. As a lover, I need to be bold and I thrive on physical contact. I enjoy giving extravagant gifts that bring obvious pleasure to my loved one.

◆ **IN CHILDHOOD,** of all types of children, I had the most difficult time fitting into academic routine. I learn by doing and experiencing, rather than by listening and reading. I need physical involvement in the learning process and am motivated by my own natural competitive nature and sense of fun.

9100

YOUR CHARACTER

Figure 4

I seek knowledge and understanding
◆ **Analytical, Global, Conceptual** ◆
I live life by my own standards
◆ **Cool, Calm, Collected** ◆
I need explanations and answers
◆ **Inventive, Logical, Perfectionistic** ◆
I value intelligence, insight, fairness, and justice
◆ **Abstract, Hypothetical, Investigative** ◆
I am a natural non-conformist, a
visionary, a problem solver

◆ **AT WORK,** I am conceptual and an independent thinker. For me, work is play. I am drawn to constant challenge in careers, and like to develop models, explore ideas, or build systems to satisfy my need to deal with the innovative. Once I have perfected an idea, I prefer to move on, leaving the project to be maintained and supported by others.

◆ **IN LOVE,** I prefer to let my head rule my heart. I dislike repetition, so it is difficult for me to continuously express feelings. I believe that once feelings are stated, they are obvious to a partner. I am uneasy when my emotions control me; I want to establish a relationship, leave it to maintain itself, and turn my energies back to my career.

◆ **IN CHILDHOOD,** I appeared to be older than my years and focused on my greatest interests, achieving in subjects that were mentally stimulating. I was impatient with drill and routine, questioned authority, and found it necessary to respect teachers before I could learn from them.

9100

YOUR CHARACTER

I need to follow rules and respect authority
◆ **Loyal, Dependable, Prepared** ◆
I have a strong sense of what is
right and wrong in life
◆ **Thorough, Sensible, Punctual** ◆
I need to be useful and to belong
◆ **Faithful, Stable, Organized** ◆
I value home, family, and tradition
◆ **Caring, Concerned, Concrete** ◆
I am a natural preserver, a parent, a helper

◆ **AT WORK,** I provide stability and can maintain organization. My ability to handle details and to work hard make me the backbone of many organizations. I believe that work comes before play, even if I must work overtime to complete the job.

◆ **IN LOVE,** I am serious and tend to have traditional, conservative views of both love and marriage. I want a mate who can work along with me, building a secure, predictable life together. I demonstrate love and affection through the practical things I do for my loved ones.

◆ **IN CHILDHOOD,** I wanted to follow the rules and regulations of the school. I understood and respected authority and was comfortable with academic routine. I was the easiest of all types of children to adapt to the educational system.

9100

YOUR CHARACTER

busy playing with the materials that they never quite get around to the planning part, but that's okay since they enjoy winging their skit anyway.

- Meanwhile, the industrious group with a preponderance of responsible golds has planned their presentation to the last detail, sorted through the materials, chosen one or two items and cleaned up their workspace before the planning time is up. They watch the chaos in the orange corner with growing dismay.
- The group with mostly blue personalities often sings its way through the activity, and invariably their poster will be illustrated with hearts, flowers, musical notes and peace signs.
- One of the activities is for the group to select a song title that best illustrates their style. I've yet to see a group with a lot of green personalities that didn't select Kermit the Frog's "It's not easy being green" as one choice. The greens have the most difficulty with the group task since, characteristically, they prefer working on their own.

Strength in diversity

Afterwards, when we ask students to comment on the activities, it's obvious that they've picked up on the concept of the True Colors® program, which honours diversity as a strength in any group. They can see why teachers might want to structure co-operative groups that include students with strengths in a variety of colours: a little gold organization, some blue harmony, a smattering of task-oriented green and a dollop of orange vitality makes for a well-balanced team. They also walk away with a little more appreciation of the need for balanced parenting skills to keep a family of diverse personalities on track. They may even concede that Mom and Dad are exercising their gold streak rather than destroying their children's lives when they ask for a few details about where they're going and with whom!

When teachers find the same diversity of styles among their colleagues as they experience in a classroom full of kids, they are often surprised. Although all four styles will be represented in any group of teachers, a disproportionate number are likely to favour the gold approach, as we noticed earlier for Alice-style school smarts. Re-experiencing a diversity of styles helps to remind teachers that they need to plan with variety in mind. Otherwise we'll probably continue to see a higher percentage of dropouts among some groups of students — especially among those with a strong orange streak, who are most likely to complain that school is boring.

I was recently reminded that attention to style can have other implications as well. My partner and I were presenting a True Colors® workshop to a group of special education teachers who work with students in need of strong teacher support. Many of their students spend at least part of the school day in special classes that allow for fewer students per teacher, often with the assistance of a classroom aide as well. Still, many of them are experiencing limited school success.

At the end of the session, when we asked each participant to share a new idea the workshop had prompted, one teacher said that True Colors® gave her a different way of thinking about the needs of the students in her classroom. Because she was preoccupied with their intellectual challenges and lumped them in her mind as the students at the lowest end of the scholastic achievement spectrum, she had forgotten that they were as varied in their styles and learning preferences as students anywhere else on that continuum.

As a matter of fact, research suggests that when adults are mindful of differences in learning, cognitive and personality styles, the students who benefit most are those who may be experiencing failure with present classroom systems. There's a maxim from the field of Total Quality Management that may have an analogy to the classroom. T.Q.M. specialists assume that when something goes terribly wrong in a production setting, 85% of the error can usually be attributed to a fault in the system, only 15% to individual error.

Although there are many differences between a classroom and a production line, I don't think it would hurt if teachers looked for that kind of ratio when students are obviously faltering. We are often quick to look for deficits within the children without thinking about whether the learning environment is working for or against them. For all kids to have an equal opportunity to meet expectations in the classroom, we must give serious thought to ways of respecting and accommodating different learning styles.

Parents can help

While teachers can learn a lot by observing their students in the classroom or by surveying them about their learning preferences, parents can also provide a good deal of valuable information about their children's individual learning styles. Indeed, that conversation should be the focus of the initial teacher-parent interview at any grade level. My son's preschool teachers could have saved themselves a lot of grief if they had asked me what would happen before they sat Christian down in front of a collection of rocks and asked him to look at them without touching. When you live with a toddler who learns everything through the senses, you anticipate that most things are going directly into his mouth.

I've also noticed from watching him at soccer practices or sharing his enthusiasm over the latest badge from Cubs that, like most people with a strong green streak, he needs to feel competent. Learning something new that doesn't come easily at first is a trial for him because of the attendant feeling of incompetence. However, if he can hang in there long enough to experience some initial success, he's fine.

If I were to share those observations with his classroom teachers, they might consider building some measures into any new learning that would allow him to see that he's making progress. Or they might remind him of previous achievements that came with practice over time. Greens also need to understand what they're doing; a little timely one-on-one coaching, or even a picture of what the end product is going to look like, can help meet that need. By sharing what I know about my child's style I'm not dictating a particular approach to instruction. I'm simply adding some pieces to the puzzle.

As a teacher on the other side of the table, I can also acknowledge the validity of the truism that no one teacher can be the best for all the children in a class. As well as having my own style as a learner, as a teacher I've developed teaching and assessing styles that feel comfortable for me. Some students may thrive in my classroom, but others will probably be challenged by my habits. Best I have some idea early on of the ones who may need the antidote. While in theory I know that I have to attend to varied styles, I will probably be more conscientious in practice if those styles are associated with particular kids in my class.

For several years now, a friend of mine who's a grade one teacher has invited the parents of her students to drop in to her classroom for an informal chat a week or so before school opens. The kids and their parents get to meet her and hear about the grade one program. The real benefit for her is all the valuable information the parents share, which she can then consider in planning for their children. She also learns a lot just from seeing the family interactions.

Unfortunately, my friend is the exception, at present, in setting aside time before school begins for meeting the parents. As parents we can take the initiative, however, by asking to meet with our child's teacher as early in the school year as possible. Even a brief phone call in the first week to introduce yourself and express an interest in hearing about your child's progress, or to provide background information, will be appreciated.

SUMMARY

Successful teaching takes into account that children differ significantly in the ways they orient themselves to learning. Parents can create more positive learning experiences at home if they also remember that all children are different. Accommodating the four basic learning styles in all learning situations — at home, at school and in the workplace — notably reduces failure.

CHAPTER 5

THE ROLE OF CONTEXT IN DEVELOPING INTELLIGENCE

My son arrived home with the news that POGS had been banned at school. Seems there were too many disputes breaking out on the playground. I'd been waiting for something like this to happen. A friend had announced that at her son's school an assembly had been held the week before to lay out the new school rules for POGS, including one against playing for keeps.

This wasn't the first time a popular fad had caused problems; two years before, marbles were the culprits. Then, too, kids had been embroiled in playground battles when someone wouldn't comply with the rules, or when an argument broke out over the fairness of a call on a play. I had listened in fascination for several weeks to stories about what was happening on the playground.

As a teacher, I was impressed by the amount of learning that accompanied the marble phenomenon:

- ratios — a math teacher's dream lesson repeated every day as kids traded marbles and negotiated their relative values according to specific criteria;
- equations — 1 dragon's eye + 1 gassy = 1 devil's eye;
- observation skills — regular tornado vs frosted tornado;
- sorting, grouping, classifying, categorizing — my son could point out all kinds of fine distinctions among marbles that all looked the same to me;
- vocabulary development — each minute difference created the need for a new name to identify the marble as belonging to a particular subset.

I suspected in my teacher heart that there was probably more authentic, meaningful learning going on out in the playground during the brief intervals when the children were released from their classrooms than happened during the rest of the school day! But all that came to an abrupt end with an executive decision from the teachers that marbles were creating too many discipline problems.

Now, two years later, we were revisiting that situation with the arrival of POGS, another traditional children's game repackaged and remarketed by enterprising adults. Seems the kids didn't learn anything from the marbles ban and the adults were having to intervene again to restore order on the playground and bring learning back into the classroom where it belongs!

Because I was a curriculum consultant for conflict resolution training at the time, I was aware that not all schools responded in the same way when a new fad stirred up action in the schoolyard. One inner-city school had tried a different approach when the marble wars began. Each class from kindergarten up was asked to select a representative to come to a meeting to discuss the marble problem with the Vice Principal. In cross-grade small-group discussions, the children analyzed the problem and brainstormed suggestions for ways of dealing with the issues.

Their initial list contained over 30 rules for ensuring that marbles would be played fairly and peacefully. When they realized that was an overwhelming number for anyone to remember, they used their skills in prioritizing to shorten the list to four basic rules. The children then introduced the rules to their classmates. They designed colourful posters and hung them at kid's-eye level near all the exit doors leading to the playground. Student monitors assumed responsibility for supervising the marble pits to ensure that everyone was following the rules and to mediate any disputes. Marble-playing resumed peacefully, without further need for adult intervention. POGS posed no problem when they hit that schoolyard. The kids knew what to do.

How learning transfers across contexts

New ideas about how people transfer their learning from one context to another should make us think again about the value of children's play and other social interactions. Once children start school, we tend to think that anything important for them to know should be taught in an academic context. For example, if we want kids to learn to solve problems, we give them lots of math problems to practise on. If we want them to learn to think critically, we ask them to write essays defending a particular thesis in a logical and convincing way. If we want them to improve their communication skills, we ask them to make presentations about topics they've researched. Usually it's our expectation (or at least hope) that the skills they are acquiring through these academic exercises will prove to be of value in other situations beyond the classroom.

If you ask parents or teachers to list their expectations for students graduating from the school system, most lists will include:

- skills for lifelong learning;
- critical and creative thinking;
- clear communication;
- personal and social responsibility;
- general knowledge about subjects included in the curriculum;
- computer literacy;
- respect for self, others and the environment;
- problem-solving and decision-making skills;
- conflict-resolution strategies.

Surprisingly, perhaps, research suggests that many students are likely to achieve mastery of these skills in a social context before they manifest them in the classroom! That might not be so surprising, however, if we think about a specific example, like language acquisition.

We were all quite proficient at speaking and listening before we ever walked through the doors of our first classroom. Listening to conversations and engaging in oral communication with other children and adults was the natural way to learn to talk. Literacy experts pay a lot of attention to signs of reading readiness in preschool children. Even those who are not yet decoding words know more about reading than we often suspect, especially if their parents have taken an active role in reading to them as toddlers. A sensitivity to grammar and sentence syntax is built right into our brains, although it may take language teachers years to drill into us a technical vocabulary for what we knew intuitively as young children.

Therefore, whenever I think about the kinds of knowledge and skills children might demonstrate at a particular stage of their intellectual development, I focus on what I see them doing in the context of a game, free play or conversation with a friend. Then the task is to consider how I can help them to transfer the learning they've acquired from that natural, familiar context to the more formal, less familiar context of the academic domain. If I ignore those other fields of learning, I may be doing both the children and myself a disservice.

The video game example

Sternberg's research on practical intelligence indicates that three factors are at play when we are in the process of acquiring expertise of any kind, whether playing second base or second fiddle, whether mastering moves on the chessboard or steps on the dance floor. Those three factors are:

Aptitude	Most of us have personal experience that confirms the belief that when you're learning something new it helps if you have natural talent. We often tend to overvalue talent.
Motivation	We sometimes underestimate the power of intrinsic motivation. It's motivation that helps us persist with difficult tasks despite initial failure.
Rehearsal	Sustained practice, too, is an important factor for successful learning. But, to be effective and motivating, practice can't be simply routine "skill and drill." Learners need increasing challenge and complexity and the opportunity to transfer acquired skills to new contexts.

A few years ago I was asked to present a session for an audience of elementary and secondary school teachers at a conference on creativity organized by a local faculty of education. During the session, I asked the teachers to think about the learning opportunities they provided in their classroom that combined those three essential features for mastering a new skill. There was a lengthy silence. Then a grade three teacher blurted out, "I can't think of anything I do in the classroom, but I think I finally understand Nintendo!"

Her comment came right at the height of the video-game debate. I had overheard numerous discussions among teachers and parents about the "video-game menace" that would turn children into zombies or, worse, reduce reading scores on standardized tests. Yet here was a teacher willing to re-evaluate what children might potentially learn about learning while helping those inveterate plumbers, Mario and Luigi.

It's interesting to think about the relationship between video games and research on kids' willingness to persist in applying problem-solving strategies when confronted with challenges like word problems in math. One of the differences often cited between Japanese and North American students is that, when faced with a challenging math problem, Japanese kids assume that persistence will pay off in the end, whereas their North American counterparts are more likely to assume that, if you don't get an answer right off the bat, you might as well quit and go on to the next question. These contrasting assumptions may explain a lot about the amount of actual time on task for the two groups and the perceived superiority of Japanese students in math.

Yet parents can certainly testify to the amount of time kids willingly devote to the mastery of each succeedingly complex level of the latest game. Not only will they persist in replaying each level until they are satisfied, but they're also quite dogged and resourceful in accessing necessary information, especially if it's secret codes that make games like Mortal Combat even gorier.

Consider what even young kids learn about the support services available for a user of new technology. They quickly discover that there are specialized magazines and reference books, hotline numbers for round-the-clock assistance, and a large information network of friends, or friends-of-friends, just a phone call or visit away. The trick is to figure out what it is you need to know. Eavesdropping on my son's calls to Nintendo's hotline in Washington State (after he's assured me that he's exhausted every free source of information), I'm amazed by his ability to formulate precise, detailed questions that get the most information in the least time. Are these kids going to have problems with the newest version of Windows or feel overwhelmed by technological change?

I'm struck by the contrast between my child's experience and the findings of research on adult learning. Most adults experience incredible frustration in trying to meet their learning needs. They have difficulty finding the resources that answer their questions. When they try to arrange learning partnerships with mentors, they often end up feeling as if they've lost control over their own learning in the process. Even the first step — being willing to admit ignorance and ask for help — is beyond many adults. Yet I often see children negotiating with teenagers, or even adults, on an equal footing because of a shared interest in a particular game challenge.

And these are relatively simple games. Think about the possibilities for higher-order thinking as children graduate to more sophisticated simulation games like Myst or Sim City, which require extensive planning, monitoring and notemaking, and the sorting and synthesizing of relevant information. Next time you're tempted to revoke your kid's playing privileges, stop and think about all the learning that might be lost.

What frustrates me, however, is that I don't usually see Christian taking what he knows in the video arcade and applying it in the world of the classroom. When he's assigned a research project, for example, I see little evidence of his skill in formulating good questions. He doesn't think about what he already knows about the topic and what he would like to know. Even if he does acquire some interesting new information or insights, he isn't motivated to take that information and use it in meaningful ways.

Having researched an endangered species, for example, he wouldn't automatically think about what he might do to address the environmental issue or to find out more about what others are doing in response to the threat. Nope. Project's done. On to the next.

A study of Brazilian street kids

Sternberg and Wagner's collection of essays on this topic, *Mind in Context,* includes a chapter about Brazilian street children. As in most Third World countries, the survival of many urban families in Brazil depends upon the income generated by children as young as five working as street vendors. Formal education is a luxury families can't afford. Their children's day is one of ongoing negotiation as they barter their products and services with tourists, performing numerous arithmetic calculations without benefit of calculators, or even paper and pencil. They must be proficient in determining prices and making change. Yet put these same children into a classroom and administer a paper-and-pencil math test and they perform abysmally.

The reverse is also true. When school children who scored quite well on classroom math tests were put into a simulated street-vending situation, they did as poorly in that context as their Brazilian counterparts did in the classroom.

So what does this study mean for parents and teachers? First, we should be very cautious about making hasty generalizations about what children can and can't do academically. What they can do in and out of school may be quite different since, in general, learners don't easily transfer what they learn in one context to another. In fact, the ability to do so is one of the distinguishing features of intellectual brilliance.

It should be no surprise, then, that a child can practise active-listening skills in the classroom and still become involved in a playground fracas because of a misunderstanding over what another kid said. Teachers who've spent hours drilling grammar rules may find themselves repeatedly correcting the same common errors in the children's writing: run-on sentences, sentence fragments, lack of correct paragraphing. Give a teacher a nickel for every time he or she puts an apostrophe in "its" or separates "alot" into two words and most could retire before the need for bifocals sets in!

Before we're too hard on the kids, though, let's think about how difficult it is for us, as adults, to apply what we've learned. I might be a great decision-maker on the job and still find out at the end of the month that I haven't made bankbook-balancing choices when I allocated the family budget. We may teach interpersonal skills as consultants and still find ourselves yelling at our own kids. Divorce counsellors have failed marriages. Doctors take a break from their appointments for a coffee and cigarette.

All this suggests that we should be realistic when we expect children to be competent in many areas of performance. We shouldn't be surprised when their learning in one area doesn't transfer naturally to another. We need to work with them specifically to find ways of bringing about that kind of transfer.

The second point to remember is that the classroom isn't the only context in which children can demonstrate their learning. In fact, for some kids it may be the one place they are least likely to appear competent. Secondary school teachers who have been involved in co-operative education programs that combine classroom instruction with on-the-job experience frequently comment on how their perceptions of their students' abilities, motivation and attitude have changed as a result of seeing them in a "real world" context. Parents may be shocked when their teenage son or daughter, who spends more time on the phone than on homework, is chosen employee of the month at the local take-out restaurant as a result of hard work, motivation and cheerful customer service. Yes, these are the same children, but the context isn't home or the classroom.

Parents, what contexts are most pleasant for your child? Will she practise basketball drills for hours? Will he volunteer to babysit the neighbours' two-year-old and have the toddler in stitches with his clowning? Does Scouting provide opportunities for leadership and skill-building through the badge program? The church choir, a dance class, a hobby bench, the local mall, quiet moments alone with a favourite author or a new set of watercolour paints — what might an observer learn about your child's learning in each of these contexts? Isn't it fascinating that a daycare centre or a kindergarten classroom would seem inadequate without its painting corner, sandbox and miniature post office and yet we are often quite satisfied to confine older children to their desks and chairs and assess their learning in that impoverished environment?

Fortunately, there are many teachers who work hard to enrich the classroom context. Visiting their classroom may leave you thinking you're somewhere else: the stock exchange, a publishing company, a design studio, a theatre, a courtroom. Or you might even find the room empty; the class may be visiting the real thing. For the children lucky enough to have one of those extraordinary teachers, the classroom will be the world itself.

Finally, we must also be mindful of studies suggesting that, when the expectations and cultures of home and school are similar, children are more likely to adjust to school routines easily and find connections between the two worlds. When these two worlds work in isolation (unfortunately, at times, at cross-purposes), some students will suffer. All the more reason why parents and teachers must see themselves as partners supporting children at school, at home and in the other areas of the community where learning opportunities await them.

SUMMARY

Children acquire new knowledge and skills in the natural, familiar context of games and other social interactions. Acquiring expertise requires a combination of aptitude, motivation and rehearsal. We need to provide opportunities for children to acquire expertise in the classroom, but at the same time we must recognize that learning occurs in other contexts as well. Our task is to assist the transfer of their learning from one context to another.

CHAPTER 6

ASK SMARTER QUESTIONS, GET SMARTER ANSWERS

Several years ago I was working with a class of adults in a course on critical and creative thinking. A couple of months into the program I invited a colleague to come to the class as guest speaker on a learning method called Superlearning. About halfway through the class, I suddenly noticed something was happening: my students were interrupting the lecture to ask questions. Once I noticed this, I started recording who was asking the questions and the nature, purpose or type of the questions they were asking.

I used Bloom's taxonomy to determine if the question was:

- asking for additional information;
- clarifying the listener's understanding of a point being made;
- suggesting an application or extension of the idea;
- analyzing a concept by breaking it down;
- synthesizing the student's experience with a point from the lecture, or suggesting a connection with something said previously;
- evaluating an idea.

When I went over my notes I found that, without having been prompted to ask questions, every one of the students had asked at least one. The purposes of their questions were varied and, in retrospect, contributed a lot to the lecture. It had been a highly interactive session with lots of interest and enthusiasm for the topic. It had been fun for the presenter too; he was pleased by the students' desire to know where they could get more information about Superlearning.

Why was this a surprise? Well, according to research, this shouldn't have happened. A recognized authority on questioning, J.T. Dillon, points out that the higher up you go in the grades, the fewer questions you find students asking. In many classrooms, only one or two students are responsible for 95% of the questions asked and responded to. (Students are less likely to ask questions in school than out of school too — an alarming fact, given that school is supposed to be the place where learning occurs.)

This was also a departure from the usual model of classroom interaction where teachers ask the questions and students supply the "right" answers. If you listen to a playback of a lot of class discussions, you might think you're in a time warp hearing Jack Webb interrogate a witness on *Dragnet*: "Just the facts, Ma'am." In that model there's not usually much higher-level thinking being elicited. At best, 20% of the teacher's questions actually require students to think — the other 80% require factual recall or basic comprehension.

What questioning strategies would be more appropriate, then? Ideally, there should be:

- a shift from teacher-generated to student-generated questions;
- more emphasis on open-ended questions that promote different responses rather than one right answer;
- higher-order questions that generate thinking that's more speculative and profound.

Did you ask a good question today, Izzy?

That's the kind of thinking that characterizes Nobel Prize-winning physicist Isidor I. Rabi, who claims that his mother's influence was the foundation for his career as a scientist. While other parents asked the usual "What did you learn in school today?" question, his mother greeted him with "Did you ask a good question today, Izzy?"

According to John Barell in *Teaching for Thoughtfulness*, if we want more Izzies in the classroom, teachers have to refine their questioning strategies so they provide good models for their students. They also have to actively teach the art of asking questions. Some teachers post question cues around the classroom to act as prompts for themselves and their students. Others use a model called the Q-matrix, which provides question stems that even primary-age children can use to formulate everything from simple factual questions of the *who? what? where? when?* type to more complex *what if?* questions that lead to predicting and other higher-order thinking. The Q-matrix also comes in handy for observing children's questioning behaviours. Parents might want to use the sample in Figure 5 to monitor their children the next time they are engaged in conversation with a friend or another adult.

Figure 5

1. WHAT IS?	2. WHERE/ WHEN IS?	3. WHICH IS?	4. WHO IS?	5. WHY IS?	6. HOW IS?
7. WHAT DID?	8. WHERE/ WHEN DID?	9. WHICH DID?	10. WHO DID?	11. WHY DID?	12. HOW DID?
13. WHAT CAN?	14. WHERE/ WHEN CAN?	15. WHICH CAN?	16. WHO CAN?	17. WHY CAN?	18. HOW CAN?
19. WHAT WOULD?	20. WHERE/ WHEN WOULD?	21. WHICH WOULD?	22. WHO WOULD?	23. WHY WOULD?	24. HOW WOULD?
25. WHAT WILL?	26. WHERE/ WHEN WILL?	27. WHICH WILL?	28. WHO WILL?	29. WHY WILL?	30. HOW WILL?
31. WHAT MIGHT?	32. WHERE/ WHEN MIGHT?	33. WHICH MIGHT?	34. WHO MIGHT?	35. WHY MIGHT?	36. HOW MIGHT?

Using the matrix, parents and teachers can discuss the children's use of questioning in the classroom. How frequently do they ask questions of the teacher or of other students? Where do their questions tend to fall on the matrix? Do they ask questions at all levels, especially *why?* and *how?* questions that prompt analysis, specificity and more elaborate answers?

Parents can use the graph to analyze their own questioning too. Do your after-school or dinner-table conversations sound like Twenty Questions? Do you find you're getting a lot of yes-or-no, grunt-or-shrug responses when you try to discover what's happening in your child's life? Then try catching the kid off guard with some questions that are a bit more creative. Here are a few possibilities to get you started:

- What did you learn today that surprised you?
- How might what you learned at school today help you in the future?
- Here's a problem I had today. Have you learned anything at school that could have helped me?
- If you could have studied anything you wanted at school today, what would that have been? Why would that have been more exciting than what you did study?
- And of course, in honour of Mrs. Rabi: Did you ask a good question today?

Taking kids' questions seriously

Parents' responses to their children's questions have an incredible influence on the children's intellectual development. In a recent article published in the educational journal *Phi Delta Kappan*, Sternberg identifies seven levels of response parents typically make to their children's questions. Each level carries a very different message about what it means to be smart.

Rejecting/ignoring the question

Child	Why is the sky blue?
Parent	Isn't it past your bed time?
Message	When we ignore their questions or change the subject

without acknowledging them, we send children the message that they shouldn't bother asking questions because they're irrelevant or unworthy of a reply. If this is our usual response, kids very quickly stop asking. In the worst cases, the questions are treated with contempt or sarcasm, leaving the children feeling stupid and afraid to admit there's something they don't understand. Older students have often had the humiliating experience of being ridiculed by a teacher or by other students in the class when they asked what seemed to them a reasonable question. It takes a lot of work to undo that harm and get kids to risk the questions that need to be asked.

Restating questions as facts

Child	Why are some people smarter than others?
Parent	Good question. Some people are smarter because they aren't dumb.
Message	One step up from the previous level because at least it's O.K. to ask the question. However, it doesn't take a rocket scientist to get the message that questions don't necessarily lead to new information. This is still a pretty minimalist response and doesn't indicate much curiosity on the parent's part!

Ignorance is bliss

Child	Where do babies come from?
Parent	Grandma says the stork brings them.
Message	If this is your usual way of shuffling off answers, don't be surprised if your child gets the message that "I don't know" absolves a person of the need to think. The child's request for information is still not being taken seriously; there's no real attempt to engage together in exploring the question.

Let's find out

Child	What's the tallest building in the world?

Parent	Information like that changes all the time. Where could we go for an up-to-date answer to that question?
Message	Even if we don't have the answer on the tip of our tongue, we can take an active role in meeting our need for information. The child also starts to get the idea that knowing where to go to find an answer might be more important than being able to recall the facts.

There's more than one answer

Child	Where did all the dinosaurs go?
Parent	Scientists have lots of different theories about that. Why don't we find out what some of them think and then we can add some of our own ideas.
Message	The good messages here are that questions hold possibilities for exploring different points of view, that adults don't always agree on the answers to questions, that it may be helpful to consider other people's ideas before coming to our own decisions about what we think, that even children may have original ideas to contribute, and that a good question deserves time for consideration instead of an immediate response.

How could we evaluate our ideas?

Child	Can dogs see colours?
Parent	I don't know. What makes you think that maybe they can?
Child	When I put the dog's dinner in the blue bowl he eats it all up, but if I use the red bowl, sometimes he hardly touches it.
Parent	Is that enough proof, or would we need more information to decide if it's the colour of the bowl that the dog prefers?
Message	When we have questions we can use strategies for developing our own answers, including gathering data and evaluating the results. We can act as researchers.

Let's put it to the test

Child	You know that poem about the shadow?
Parent	"I have a little shadow that goes in and out with me"?
Child	Yes. I wonder when my shadow is the longest.
Parent	I wonder too. How could we design a way to find out?
Message	Thinking about our reading is a great way to generate questions. Then we can use our critical and creative thinking skills to find answers to those questions. This level of response creates many opportunities for what author Eleanor Duckworth calls "the having of wonderful ideas."

Throughout his article, Sternberg suggests that, as parents, we could be doing a lot more to enhance the frequency and quality of our children's questions by monitoring our own responses. Far too often we slough them off with a hasty response that may satisfy the child's immediate need for information but doesn't do much to promote thoughtfulness.

Wait time

A strategy that many teachers have been taught can help all adults to avoid the thoughtless quick answer. This is called "wait time." Research has shown that an overly hasty response, either after asking a child a question or before responding to a child's question, doesn't honour the need for time that good thinking requires. According to Barell (p.84), teachers typically pause only two or three seconds after asking a student a question. If the child doesn't immediately start to reply, the teacher frequently does one of three things:

- redirects the question to someone else;
- repeats or rewords the question;
- answers the question himself or herself!

The first response often backfires. Kids either get the idea that if you just wait a second or two the teacher will let you off the hook and you won't have to think, or the even worse notion that you're stupid and have to be rescued if you can't summon an immediate response.

In other words, good thinking means fast thinking.

The second is a bit more helpful, but it can still give a mixed message: you don't have to listen the first time because the teacher will say it again. It also reinforces the idea that answers should follow immediately.

The third response is the worst, it seems to me, because it demonstrates a total lack of confidence in the child. It's as if teachers are, like radio announcers, afraid of dead air time.

The benefits of waiting

When teachers pause and wait for up to five seconds after the question (for more complex questions as long as 10 seconds), amazing things can happen:

- Students respond with longer, better-developed answers.
- More students volunteer answers, not just the two or three who always have their hands up.
- Teachers hear "I don't know" less often.
- Students demonstrate more confidence in their ability to answer questions.
- Students are more likely to provide speculative answers because they don't get the message that they have to be 100% sure in order to venture an idea.
- Students use each others' responses to help in gathering and comparing information.
- Students can draw more inferences from the facts presented to them.
- Students ask more of their own questions.
- Students who are shy or slower to respond to questions participate more fully.
- Best of all, teachers can stop answering their own questions!

Silence is both an opportunity and a challenge, not only for asking children questions but also for responding to theirs. Taking a few seconds to think before responding gives us time to formulate a more thoughtful response. Nothing is more empowering to a child (or an adult, for that matter) than to see someone else taking his or her questions seriously. So try the wait-time strategy the next time you ask or respond to a question and see how it works for you.

Observing a thoughtful teacher in action

I saw this respect for children's questions modelled by a master teacher when I had a chance to spend about an hour one morning in her grade four classroom. When I arrived, the children were working in small groups studying a thematic unit on air. They had been "doing" air for almost a month but were nowhere near done with the topic.

One group was designing kites. They had reference books from the library and were making sketches and talking about their plans. They consulted the teacher as she and I were making our rounds: what materials could they use to construct the frames for their kites, since the classroom supply of balsa wood was gone? The teacher paused to think and then asked the children if they remembered seeing a display in the school featuring objects that were both light and sturdy. Someone remembered a construction project the grade six class had done. What did they use for their supports? Paper rolled into tubes. The teacher wondered aloud if that class might have some ideas that would be helpful. Before we knew it, one of the kids was off to borrow an expert from the grade six class.

In the hallway another group was designing a mural showing different uses of air: windmills, hot-air balloons, etc. One of the boys was mixing paint and came to ask the teacher if he had the right shade for the background. She paused, then asked a series of clarifying questions: What is the effect you want for the background? How is it going to relate to the objects that other people in your group are going to paint? How could you experiment with different shades to test the effect? Off went the boy with some new questions for the group.

As we toured the room, I noticed a birdcage sitting on one of the desks. It had a sparrow inside. On the way to school, one of the children had found the bird lying on the sidewalk and rescued it. At recess time the children had looked for some worms and brought them in for the bird's morning snack. Now a little girl approached the teacher to ask if she thought they should let the bird go. Again the teacher paused to think before responding.

Teacher Why are you thinking that we should let the bird go?

Girl I've been watching it for a while and I think maybe its wing isn't broken like we thought it was this morning.

Teacher What have you seen that makes you think this?

Girl It seems to be trying to fly. It's up near the top of the cage fluttering its wings.

Teacher I wonder if anyone else in the class has an opinion about what we should do with the bird?

Unprompted, the child took a piece of paper, drew a line down the middle and proceeded to conduct an informal survey of the class: Yes, we should let the bird go; No, we should keep the bird in the classroom. She arrived back a bit later to present her survey results to the teacher. The teacher looked at the numbers and asked her to summarize what the class was thinking.

Student Maybe this is a mother bird that has babies in her nest. If she can fly and we keep her here, then maybe her babies will die because there is no one to bring them food. But if we decide to let her go and she can't fly, then a cat might get her. We think maybe we should watch her for the rest of the day and then, when we have our class meeting at the end of the day, we can decide whether to keep the bird or let it go.

In the hour I spent in that room, even life-and-death questions were turned back to the children for their thinking. Not once did the teacher give a quick response to a question. Every question was considered thoughtfully and used as an opportunity to challenge the child to explore his or her own thinking more fully. The children's expertise in finding appropriate strategies to help them generate answers to their questions was valued and encouraged. I left feeling that I had learned as much as those lucky children, whose teacher understood her role in facilitating the development of intellectual rigour in the classroom.

I was curious, however, about how the parents of those students felt about what their children were experiencing in the class. Many of them were recent immigrants from countries where more traditional, authoritarian teaching styles are the norm. How did they respond to a classroom organized to facilitate small-group learning when they were familiar with desks in straight rows? If their experience with school included a teacher at the front of the room who asked the questions and drilled "correct" responses, what did they make of a teacher who deferred to the children in both asking and answering questions?

When she described one of her meetings with a group of parents, I realized that she was no different in her interactions with them than she was with the students. She began her presentation by asking them for comments about what she was doing in the classroom: What feelings were the children showing when they talked about school? Were they enthusiastic about coming to class? Did they volunteer information about what was being studied? How did the parents feel about the quality of the work their children were producing? When they looked at the children's portfolios, did they see evidence of growing skills and knowledge?

After she had given the parents an opportunity to share their comments, she showed slides of their kids in the classroom, explaining the methods she was using for organizing their study, showing the relationship between her planning and the results the children were achieving, inviting questions and critiques of her work. Her respect for the parents' need to know and understand what was happening in the classroom was exemplary. I went back to my own classroom with a clearer sense of the work to be done with both students and parents if a teacher wants to promote high-level thinking.

Some questions are for life

If we are interested, as parents, in promoting good thinking, then let's find new ways to get the questions flowing. Most of us laugh about the phase our children went through when the day was filled with questions and "Why?" seemed to be the immediate response to everything we said. Instead of being relieved that those challenging days are gone, perhaps we need to consider how we might revive that boundless curiosity.

It's interesting to consider that, when biographers research the early lives of men and women who have made notable contributions in the sciences and arts, they often discover that the questions that led these people to new discoveries and achievements first arose during childhood. Fortunately for many of the young Einsteins, family members and friends took their questions seriously, providing them with materials and resources, including toys, that allowed them to explore their questions in more depth.

When you stop to think about it, can you remember questions you had as a child that might well have been an early indication of an area of knowledge that's still of interest to you as an adult? What questions do your children seem to keep coming back to? How responsive have you been to their curiosities? Are there additional ways of assisting them with their explorations?

Personally, I'm hoping that my son continues with what seems to be a recurring interest in precious gems. When I noticed that there was a television program featuring the history of some of the world's most famous jewels, I suggested that we watch the show together. Then a few days later there was an article in the Sunday paper about the dangers a local scientist had encountered when she went to Colombia to study the huge treasure trove of emeralds that, according to conventional geological theories, shouldn't be there. That brought together two of his interests — jewels and desperados.

He's very keen now on the idea of taking a trip to Thailand, since it looked from the TV show as if you could buy whole bags of jewels there for a couple of dollars. He's obviously ready to move on from the minerals and semi-precious stones we've picked up on vacations and at museums to the real stuff, and I'm counting on the possibility that somewhere in this discovery process Mom is going to strike it rich with a birthday present the size of the Ritz! I'm taking his question about how we can finance a trip to Thailand's jewel bazaar very seriously.

SUMMARY

Teachers and parents need to refine their questioning techniques to provide better models for children. Because our responses to their questions have an incredible influence on their intellectual development, we must always take our children's questions seriously and answer them thoughtfully, in ways that have a positive effect on their view of themselves and of learning. Often, childhood questions predict lifelong interests.

CHAPTER 7

JUST WHOSE PROJECT IS THIS?

When I was chatting with a group of students one day about their almost-due book report, it became clear that about half of them hadn't even finished reading their book. They were all quite confident their reports would be ready, of course, although they were a little hazy about how this miracle was going to happen.

I asked one student, as an example, how many pages he had left to read in his book and what his average reading speed was: how many pages per hour, max? Then we did a rough graphic organizer to break down his available time into half-hour segments, from when school got out until the time he normally went to bed. When we'd filled in all the stuff he was already committed to do — band practice, and dinner, and an hour on the phone talking to friends, and the TV shows he *had* to watch — he was amazed to find how little time there was left to finish the book, never mind write the report.

I want to make it clear that this was a bright, motivated group of students, not a bunch of slugs. They had every intention of doing whatever work their teacher assigned. So why were they in this pickle? Probably because:

- they hadn't been taught the skills of project management;
- when they'd fallen behind in the past, their parents had bailed them out;
- since teachers don't want to see kids fail, they regularly allow extensions.

What substantiates those theories? My own experience, and I know I'm not alone! I've met parents who are also teachers who will confess, in private, that they did indeed construct their child's Mayan pyramid from sugar cubes over an entire weekend because:

- it was their idea in the first place;

- the kid got frustrated because it was too hard;
- after spending all that money on sugar cubes they didn't want to see them go to waste;
- they had to top last year's project (the lava-belching volcano);
- they were more interested in Mayan pyramids than the child would ever be;
- they always wanted to be an architect;
- they wanted it done right!

Usually by about grade four, teachers begin assigning projects that culminate in a written report, along with some form of visual display. Even with the unfortunate trend toward eliminating or drastically reducing teacher-librarian support, it's still possible in most schools to take kids to the library and introduce them to the basic research skills: locating information via encyclopedias, books and, increasingly, CD-ROMs and the Internet. However, teaching them how to determine what information they need and what to do with it once they've collected it isn't always part of the lesson. As a result, the students develop misconceptions about the purpose and the process of individual and collective research. And when you don't really understand what you're doing, or even why you're doing it, procrastination may be the most logical response. So, if we're going to assign projects, we need to teach project management as well as research skills.

A few years ago I was heading up a curriculum writing project that involved collaboration with teacher representatives from a number of school boards. In preparation, curriculum project managers and lead writers were sent to a three-day workshop on project management. Even as a teacher, this was all new to me. I understood how it could help to ensure that the team met the four-week deadline for a first-draft document, but my teacher mind wondered how I had managed to spend so many years as a student without already being introduced to these concepts and strategies. The idea of starting with the end in mind and working backwards to determine the steps and the timing needed to meet that goal would have helped me enormously. As an adult, I still struggle to overcome a mindset that makes initiating and sustaining projects hard work. As teachers, we need to learn or refine the skills of project management so we can teach them more effectively to our students.

When I work with parents I often ask them to think about the biggest event they've ever organized, either by themselves or with others. Often it's a special occasion like a wedding or family reunion; for some it's a move from one country to another. Then we create a map of all the skills involved in planning that event. We sometimes fill a wall, especially when getting the work done involves the subtleties of delegating crummy jobs to other people without alienating their support! Or negotiating their involvement in the first place.

How did most of us learn these skills? Trial-and-error is the usual response. Would there be any merit in learning how to manage projects like these in a more systematic way? Oh, yes! When would be a good age to start? The sooner the better!

Project management

To manage projects well, students need a combination of specific skills and broader, more general models for planning. Ensuring that they have both requires collaboration among teachers across grade levels to develop a sequence for introducing, refining and reinforcing these skills. Otherwise, projects can become more complex than necessary, since different teachers have different expectations. Sometimes students can't even rely on their prior experience to help them as they struggle to meet requirements they haven't been trained for.

Gathering data

How to search for information is a good example. Teachers often require a bibliography of secondary resources — books, articles, encyclopedias, etc. — and assign marks for correct bibliographic form. Although they might provide a handout showing the students how to set up the entries, they usually don't address the thinking part of using secondary resources. So the kids rush to the library and take out a whole shelf-load of books without any idea of how they're going to use them. The concept that not all information is equally relevant or reliable isn't part of their thinking.

When I work with a classroom teacher, I often suggest taking the class to the library for a lesson on evaluating resources. We might, for example, give the students a topic from the class's project list and have them check it out in three or four different encyclopedias.

Providing a graphic organizer for them to complete helps them to analyze such things as:

- the number of pages devoted to the topic;
- the authority of the author of the article (was it an expert who wrote it or someone unnamed?);
- accompanying graphs, charts, illustrations (do they help your understanding of key information?);
- cross-references and indexes that lead to additional information elsewhere in the encyclopedia;
- footnotes that would help in tracking down other books;
- reading level of the encyclopedia (can you understand what you're reading?).

Evaluating resources is a subskill that needs to be taught explicitly, and practised, if we expect students to use secondary sources intelligently. Otherwise, we shouldn't be surprised when their projects include healthy doses of copying from books or CD-ROMs.

Last year I noticed my son downloading information directly from the Internet, thinking that his project was virtually done. All he had to add was a title page and a couple of cute drawings. He wasn't happy when I told him he was still at step one — gathering data — and that printing off pages from an encyclopedia would give his teacher no indication of his understanding of the topic he was researching. I don't think he was even clear that that's the purpose of a project: to demonstrate heightened understanding of the research topic.

Selecting subtopics

In preparing this chapter I was revisiting some of the materials our board provides to help students with their study and research skills. I give them credit for providing the material, but they've left a few enormous gaps in dealing with the subtleties of research. For example, step four in one of the step-by-step models is: "Select subtopics or key words to guide your research." It's a good idea, but how exactly do you break a topic down into subtopics?

How do you know when you've got a topic that's broad enough in scope to meet the requirements for the project but not so big that you're going to spend huge amounts of time reading and then find out that you can't use most of it? How do you avoid finding out part way through the process that you've got a neat topic but unfortunately the materials you need aren't readily available? My husband loves explaining to my son that he won a trophy in elementary school for his winning speech, grandly titled "The Earth," but as a teacher I've learned the hard way that time spent in helping students to develop a more reasonable focus for their research leads to better end products.

There are a number of different ways to teach a skill like developing subtopics. One of my favourites is a strategy called T-E-C (Target-Expand-Contract), which is part of Edward De Bono's CoRT program. In applying the technique I use a series of circles to help students identify a focus for investigation. (A similar technique is mindmapping. See page 90.)

Let's say I'm a kid and my class is doing a project on endangered species. Figure 6 shows how I might begin to identify a subtopic for my research. But that's about as far as I can go in breaking down the broad topic without doing some background research.

Now, what is it I've done? I started off with a big topic — *endangered species* — and came up with four subtopics. I found one especially interesting — *rainforest* — so I used that as my new topic and again identified four subtopics. From those I chose one — *medicinal plants* — as my new, more focused topic. This time I had to think a bit harder about subtopics, a sure sign that I was near the end of my prior knowledge. So, to go any further I'll have to search for more information.

But the process has been rewarding. By taking a few minutes to focus my topic I've rediscovered something that has some interest for me — otherwise it probably wouldn't have come to mind so readily. I probably saw a documentary or read an article sometime in the past that left me with an interesting fact tucked away in my brain: that the ingredients of some medicines used to treat illnesses like cancer come from plants that are being destroyed as more and more of the rain forest is cultivated. Usually when people think of endangered species it's animals that come to mind, as my first set of subtopics reveals. But since my past experience has brought to my attention that some plant

Figure 6

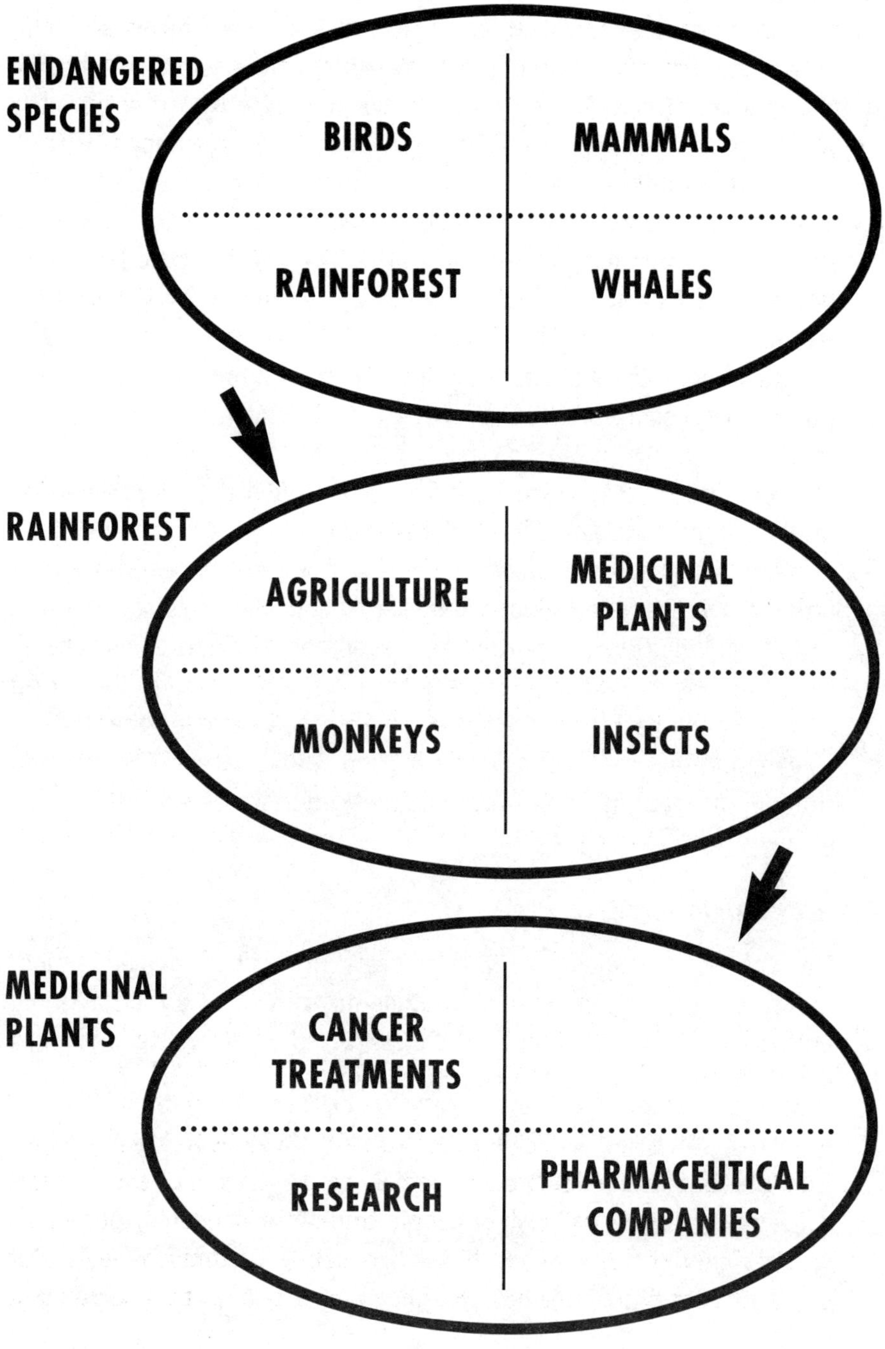
ENDANGERED SPECIES
BIRDS
MAMMALS
RAINFOREST
WHALES
RAINFOREST
AGRICULTURE
MEDICINAL PLANTS
MONKEYS
INSECTS
MEDICINAL PLANTS
CANCER TREATMENTS
RESEARCH
PHARMACEUTICAL COMPANIES

species are also threatened with extinction, my project is taking off in quite a different direction from that of my classmates.

As I proceed with my research, I might find that the four labels from my last circle establish the organization for my project. I'll begin by explaining the problem, then cite cancer treatment as a specific example, and finally move on to some of the responses, first from the pharmaceutical companies and then from concerned groups or individuals. I might even add some ideas about how students like myself can get involved, perhaps with a class fundraising project to buy a few hectares of rainforest. Or I might find that, given the time I have for the project, I need to continue trying to narrow my focus because I still have too much information. Or I might discover that I have to go back to a prior circle because my focus is too narrow, or the information is so specialized that I'm having trouble understanding what I'm reading.

The point is that when I use this process I'm thinking like a real researcher. As Sternberg often tried to explain to his graduate students at Yale, being able to identify a research topic that captures your interest *and* challenges your intellect *and* contributes something new to the field of study is what research is all about. What it's not about, even for younger students — although many have come to believe so — is simply rehashing old knowledge. Yes, students need the skills of researching and synthesizing information. But creative planning and thinking are just as important, and we do our students a real disservice when we forget that.

Project planning skills

Many of the strategies used in large-scale project management would, in simplified form, be helpful to students embarking on a classroom project. For example, together a class or co-operative small groups could:

- write a shared definition of the project, its purpose and its scope;
- develop a list of needed resources;
- create a flowchart to outline the steps of the project;
- negotiate responsibilities for specific tasks to ensure an equitable distribution of the work;

- establish timelines for completing each phase of the project;
- identify potential problems and possible solutions;
- establish responsibility for monitoring the process to ensure completion;
- develop criteria for ensuring quality in the final product.

Allocating class time for these planning discussions would prevent a lot of the predictable difficulties that students may experience when they're not clear about the teacher's expectations, the criteria by which the project will be evaluated, or the availability of resources.

A new role for parents

Within this kind of structure, teachers and parents can also negotiate their roles in supporting the students' independent learning. As a parent, I can still be actively involved — not in doing the work but in helping my child to monitor and assess the project management process. For instance, were the anticipated timelines realistic or is he falling behind schedule? Is she having difficulty accessing resources? Are other group members on task with their responsibilities? Is there a need to rethink the scope of the project?

As adults, we've all been in the position of feeling we've bitten off more than we can chew. Sometimes we decide to allocate more resources to complete the task because it's important to us. Other times we can be satisfied with scaling down our initial plans, still doing a good job but not quite such an ambitious one. Sometimes students also need to consider personal priorities and allocate their time disproportionately to certain assignments. A child might choose to do an adequate job on one assignment in order to devote extra time to another that has more relevance or interest or value to him or her. Parents can become the sounding board as the children work their way through decisions about how to manage conflicting priorities.

I know that, as a teacher, I've been guilty on occasion of forgetting that my students have peak assignment times when they have to struggle to complete several projects within a few weeks. Sometimes something has to give. I would hope that by engaging the students in the planning process we could prevent those stresses as much as possible, but there will always be conflicts. And that's O.K. There's merit, too, in learning to cope with conflicting priorities and develop contingency plans.

If teachers want to work in partnership with parents, it's important that they share information about upcoming projects and suggest ways the parents can be involved. One of the neatest ideas I've heard came from a school that replaced its traditional science fair with a family project fair. Each family designed and presented a project they had developed together. What a fabulous opportunity for teaching all partners the skills of project management before asking the children to embark on the road to independent self-directed learning!

Mindmapping

Another study skill I've introduced to students, one I'm very excited about, is a technique called *mindmapping*. Initially developed by England's Tony Buzan, it's a dynamic technique more teachers and parents should know about. (See Buzan's *Use Both Sides of Your Brain* for an explanation of the theory behind it.) Figure 7 illustrates the technique with a mindmap for this chapter of this book.

Mindmapping is a simple way of connecting words and images to enhance the retention and retrieval of information. Combined with Buzan's systematic approach to reviewing daily learning, it can help older students study for tests and examinations, and yet it's so simple that it can even be used in the primary grades. My students also found it a more interesting approach to note-taking and brainstorming than the more linear techniques they had learned before.

A few years ago I was asked by a community college teacher to do a session for his first-year students who were experiencing difficulty in their training for airplane maintenance. When I asked what skills he wanted me to address in the two-hour session, he rhymed off the following "for starters": taking lecture notes, reading comprehension, preparing for tests, and essay and report writing. I suggested mindmapping as an alternative. I asked him to lend me a copy of the course text and indicate which chapter the students would be working on when I came. It turned out that they were learning how to load an airplane.

Using Buzan's strategy, the first thing I did was to get out a blank piece of paper and mindmap everything I knew (or thought I knew)

Figure 7

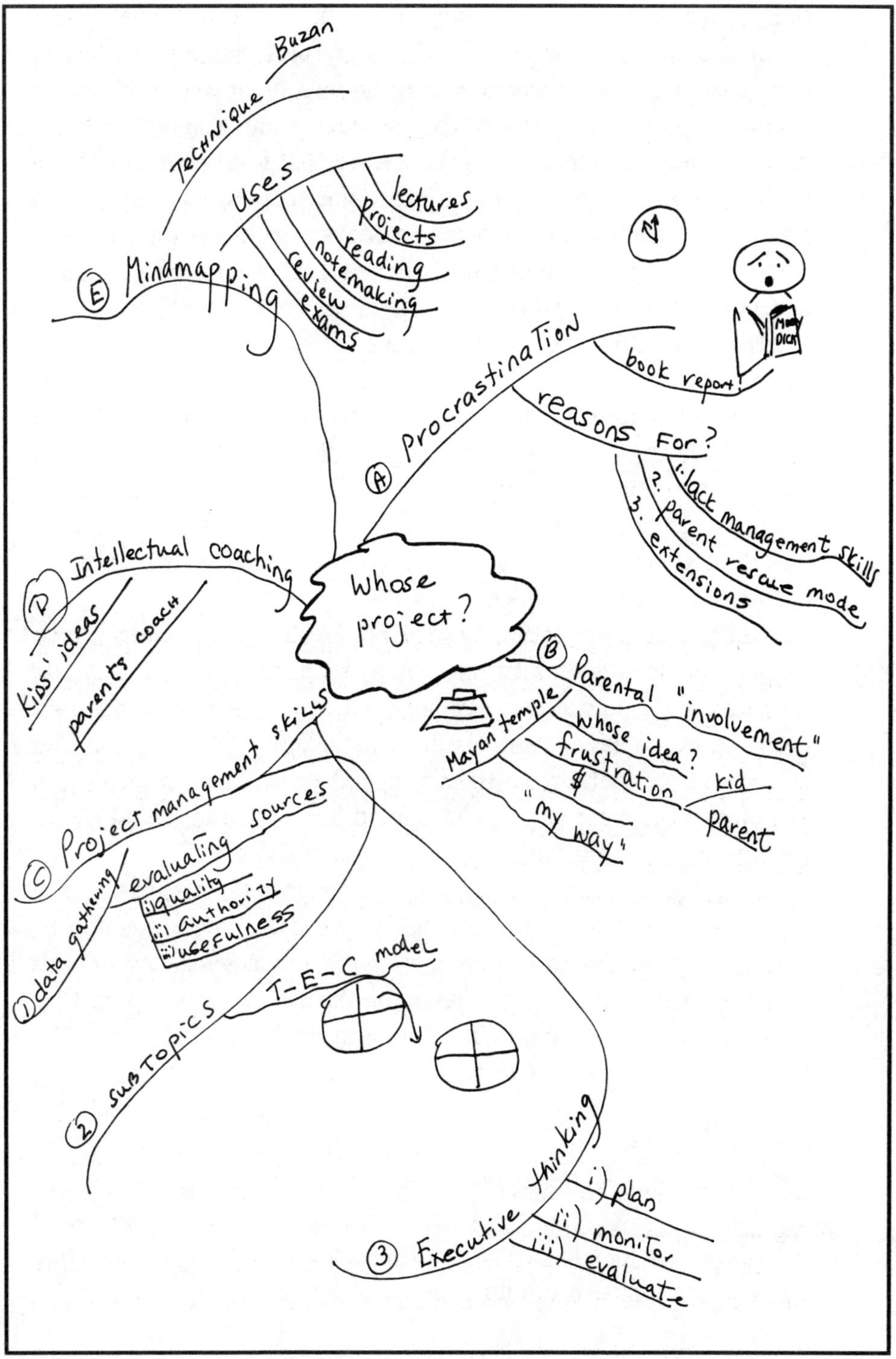
Whose project?
A Procrastination
book report
MOBY DICK
reasons for?
1. lack management skills
2. parent rescue mode
3. extensions
B Parental "involvement"
whose idea?
frustration
kid
parent
Mayan temple
$
"my way"
C Project management skills
1) data gathering
evaluating sources
i) quality
ii) authority
iii) usefulness
2) subtopics
T-E-C model
3) Executive thinking
i) plan
ii) monitor
iii) evaluate
D Intellectual coaching
kids' ideas
parents coach
E Mindmapping
uses
lectures
projects
reading
notemaking
review
exams
technique
Buzan

about loading a plane. In other words, I was accessing my prior knowledge, a good approach to learning something new. I used what I knew about a ship's cargo to predict that they probably used ballast in planes as well. I remembered a story about a flight where the attendants polled the passengers to see how many weighed over 90 kilograms because the pilot was concerned that they weren't going to make takeoff, and another about jettisoning fuel in an emergency. So I assumed that in loading a plane you have to consider the weight of passengers, cargo and fuel and that there's probably a bit of science and/or math involved in the process.

Then I went to the 30-page chapter in the textbook. First I surveyed the chapter subheadings and added them to my map. I checked out the illustrations, charts and diagrams to see what else I could learn about the topic before actually wading into the text. A good plan, because once I hit the technical stuff — the equations and formulas — without that big picture I would have been lost. Nevertheless, in a little over an hour I had a reasonable map of the chapter all on one large piece of paper.

I began my presentation by showing the students a brief clip from a video on coping with difficult people, asking them to take notes as they normally would. Several volunteered to jot their notes on overheads so we could compare the information they included. Then we looked at those notes from the standpoint of another classmate who had missed the presentation and wanted to borrow them. How useful would they be as a record of the key ideas of the video?

All of the students had used a point-form style for their notes, with a few variations. But the class quickly agreed that they wouldn't be easy for anyone else to use because the main ideas didn't stand out from the details and the organization on the page was confusing. They were also quite messy because the note-takers had to keep pace with the video — which was no different from the usual classroom situation, since their instructor often lectured non-stop for three hours while the class tried to keep up. The students had to learn and remember this information not only for the regular class tests and examinations, but also for a government certification examination they had to take before they could get jobs in their field. They knew that they had to figure out a better approach to information management.

Using the video clip again, I demonstrated mindmapping as an alternative approach to note-making. Part of the technique is paying attention to the way the information is being structured by the presenter and using those verbal cues to organize the notes. Key information is highlighted by being put in the centre of the page; you move out from it with the finer details. Once you've got the basic map you can highlight related ideas by adding colour, and reinforce key words and phrases by incorporating simple drawings.

The students picked up the idea immediately. Many were strong visual, hands-on learners, and that's why lectures and textbooks weren't their favourite mode of learning. They also found that this technique helped to keep them from drifting off, as they sometimes did when they were just listening.

The real selling feature, however, was presenting them with the chapter from their text. I explained that if they took the time to pre-read the text and make their mindmap before the lecture, then they could listen and highlight the map to indicate the information the instructor emphasized. They wouldn't need to try to keep pace with three hours of talking; they could simply add any new information that wasn't already in the text. And if they got really smart, they could do the mindmapping together or divy up the chapters.

The response from the class: why hadn't I come in September and how much for the mindmap? One chapter is my gift, guys. The rest is up to you.

Other uses for mindmapping

We then discussed Buzan's suggestions for using mindmaps for study. He recommends sitting down with a blank paper the day after the initial lecture and trying to reproduce the map from memory. Then you compare it with the original, focusing on the information that failed to transfer into longterm memory. Review becomes much more efficient this way, because each time you return to the map it's with the purpose of reinforcing what you forgot. With practice, this procedure becomes even quicker and more effective.

I also showed them a number of additional uses for the technique I'd learned from other authors, including Joyce Wycoff and Nancy Margulies. For example, with elementary and secondary students I often use it as a reading and prewriting strategy. Mindmapping is a great way to find out quickly if you have enough to say on any topic before you start writing — if you can't generate a fairly detailed map, you'd better pick another topic or prepare to do some background research. Students can also use the map to sequence their ideas so they already have the basic outline of their composition or essay in mind as they begin writing. (This is similar to the T-E-C technique. See page 86.)

Mindmaps are a great help in structuring presentations as well. I've never been able to use the little index cards that many teachers require kids to prepare before making oral presentations. I'd much rather put up a mindmapped poster or overhead and talk to it. Mapping works well for any kind of planning and for any time you need to keep an eye on both the big picture and the details of an activity.

Buzan's system also really helps students who are prone to test anxiety. I've often seen kids in the hallway before a test or exam wildly flipping through their notes because they're afraid of drawing a blank as soon as they're handed the test paper. Instead, sitting quietly looking at a couple of mindmaps that highlight the key information to be tested helps kids to feel focused and prepared. Research shows that under stress we're far more likely to remember pictures than words, so maps are more apt to come back under the pressure of a high-stakes test. Encountering essay examinations that include question choices can also create panic in older students, but if the technique is familiar to them they can very quickly mindmap responses to a number of questions and select the ones they're most prepared to answer.

I especially like to have my class work together periodically to create large bulletin-board mindmaps that consolidate what we've learned together. This helps the kids see connections among the various topics and themes of a program or of the school year. It also creates a sense of shared understanding and purpose and can be very motivating, since the students get a feeling for how much they've accomplished. At the same time, it gives me feedback about the connections students are making. I know very quickly what needs to be reviewed if the majority have forgotten a key concept.

In building class mindmaps, it's important to start by inviting each student to make an individual map. They can gradually consolidate their maps by working first with a partner and then in groups of four and eight. Sharing their individual and paired maps almost always results in further recall. This kind of shared mindmapping is also a great way to get the class ready for an important assessment.

Parents who understand and practise mindmapping with their children find that the technique works for themselves as well. As computers and other technical innovations give us access to more information, our data management strategies need to keep pace or we can quickly end up feeling overwhelmed. On the other hand, people who can sift through a lot of data to find key information, which they can then manipulate in creative ways, become the stars in a lot of different settings. I like the idea that the same model young children are using to enhance their learning skills in the classroom might also help Mom and Dad in managing their workload.

SUMMARY

Most students, and many adults, have never been taught the skills of project management. As a result, they develop misconceptions about the purpose and the process of research. Project management requires specific skills, like gathering data and selecting focused topics, as well as general models for planning. Mindmapping is a particularly useful study and organization skill that has wide applications for both children and adults.

CHAPTER 8

THE MAGIC OF METACOGNITION

It was an *AHA!* moment. My son, about eight, was reminiscing about a red-letter day in grade one. His class had been listening to the teacher read one of the seemingly thousands of children's stories that feature a family with both a dog and a cat when, all of a sudden, Christian realized that not all cats were female and all dogs male, as he had always thought. He had been excited by this insight but also mortified that he could have been so mistaken for so long.

He laughed when he told me about it, remembering how whenever he saw a dog he automatically looked for a nearby cat, since in his mind the two were mates. When we got home that day we looked through his library of picture books and could see how he got that idea and how he might naturally have over-generalized to arrive at his conclusion about the gender of dogs and cats. What struck me, though, was how vividly he remembered that moment of insight when he reconceptualized his original idea in light of conflicting information.

That's the magic of metacognition: thinking about your own thinking.

When we give children frequent opportunities to revisit previous experience and talk about how their understanding has grown and changed over time, these moments of insight can happen regularly. Discussions like these also remind us that children are not blank slates. Their minds are filled with fabulous memories, images and theories that must be tapped into for new learning to occur. In *The Unschooled Mind*, Gardner suggests that it's because adults usually omit this important step in the learning process that so little of academic learning actually "takes."

He believes that by age five children have developed sophisticated theories about how the world operates. Some of these, like my son's animal gender theory, are misconceptions based on limited or misunderstood experiences. And yet they are powerful; these mental connections that we forge for ourselves tend to stay with us even into adulthood. Left unchallenged, our early theories persist and are much more likely to shape our attitudes and behaviour than anything we learn in school. In some cases, our ignorance can even inoculate us against new knowledge. That's probably what we mean when we quote the maxim "A little learning is a dangerous thing."

The 50% factor

It would be nice to think that as we mature intellectually and socially we become more capable of recognizing our own illogic and the habits of thinking that no longer serve us well. And yet research suggests that for many adults this is not the case. Art Costa maintains that fewer than 50% of adults are self-reflective — that is, able to process their own thinking in ways that would allow for new insights and less habitual or stereotypical thinking. We may not realize the essential truth of the adjectives used to describe such people ("thoughtless") and their activities ("mindless"), or of the fact that certain reflective modes of thinking underlie the behaviour that we appreciate in others as "thoughtful" or "mindful."

Metacognition is not something we learn automatically, and yet the benefits inherent in a reflective approach to living and learning are incredible. In a landmark book called *Mindfulness*, Dr. Ellen Langer of Harvard University's Faculty of Medicine shares the results of her research in numerous areas, including the role that thinking plays in healthful aging and longevity.

What her studies show is that people who adopt a self-reflective approach that allows them to literally "rethink" the significance of events or impressions they originally formed show specific characteristics. They:

- live longer, healthier lives;
- experience less loss of memory as they age;
- are more creative;
- promote creativity in others, including their employees and children;
- are less likely to exhibit prejudice;
- have better success in overcoming addictions;
- are less afraid of failure;
- are more open to change.

Essentially, mindful adults feel in control of themselves and their response to whatever life throws at them. I often hear the platitude that one of the chief goals of education is to prepare students for "lifelong learning." I define that for myself as ensuring that students have the thinking strategies that characterize the minority of mindful adults.

Building metacognition into classroom instruction

What needs to change in terms of classroom practice if we want learning to truly impact on students? Here are some ideas for you to think about.

Activating prior knowledge

The first step is to activate prior knowledge and experience before introducing new concepts or skills. For instance, if the lesson is focusing on a particular skill in decision-making, like applying criteria to evaluate options, the teacher might begin by asking the children to share with a partner an example of a time when they had to make an important choice. Even very young children can usually think of a recent experience — choosing a gift for a friend, buying a family pet, even selecting an ice cream cone from the 31 flavours available. In a class discussion, the children can explore the different ways they went about making those choices. What helped? What made choosing really hard?

When I describe this process of activating prior knowledge to older students or adults, I like to use the analogy of a filing-cabinet drawer. If I'm going to store some new information, it helps if I have a system in place that's going to make it easy to both file and retrieve the information. Having one huge folder labelled "miscellaneous" might make the filing quick, but I sure am going to spend a lot of time shuffling through papers if I ever need to find that particular piece of data again. We all have a big miscellaneous file in our heads: knowledge that is basically "inert" because it went into our what-I-learned-at-school-today compartment and we've lost whatever the code was that allowed us to access it efficiently.

So, if I think for a minute about how some new piece of information is related to all the stuff I already have stored in my head, I can make a more thoughtful decision about where to place it. Sternberg, who calls this process "selective encoding," states that thinking about how information is being taken in, sorted and filed is one habit that characterizes smart people. He uses an analysis he did of how bright students approach the task of taking a standardized test to illustrate what makes this process so effective.

We often tend to associate being smart with quick thinking, but Sternberg noticed something very different about the pacing of these students. At the beginning of the test, they were much slower than the "average" student because they were spending time thinking about the questions — not just to determine the right answers but also to learn something about the types of questions: verbal analogies (*dog is to puppy as cat is to* _____), numerical sequences (*what number comes next in this series: 1, 2, 4, 7, 11,* _____), etc.

While the average test-takers treated each question discretely and maintained an unvarying pace, the better test-takers gradually picked up speed as the test progressed. They began to identify patterns in the types of questions and, once they figured out how to answer each type of question, they saved time. In other words, as they worked through the test they became test-smarter, and it was that learning process that accounted, at least in part, for their better results. They were drawing on their experience in completing prior questions to monitor and improve their performance as they went. They were selecting and encoding information in a different way from the other students taking the same test.

Promoting self-reflection

One of the things that makes bright kids shine is that they've developed metacognitive strategies. But other kids can be taught to do what those kids have picked up intuitively. Teachers can begin to address some of the gaps in achievement by:

- observing and analyzing what the capable students are doing;
- making their thinking processes explicit for the other students by naming or labelling the processes, sequencing the steps and modelling;
- providing rehearsal or practice opportunities;

- observing and providing feedback as students work through the process.

During this rehearsal stage, teachers need to take an active role in performing the four Cs:

Coaching	They need to provide suggestions or helpful hints.
Cueing	They need to keep the students on track by referring them to the sequence of steps.
Clarifying	They need to watch for indicators of misunderstanding and provide a new explanation or example.
Commenting	They need to point out to students how they are meeting the objectives of the process.

When teachers provide this kind of scaffolding for their students, they are modelling the thinking processes the students must gradually internalize to become self-reflective. Few of us will go through life like Olympic athletes with high-paid experts on the sidelines to drive us to new heights of performance. Instead, we have to monitor ourselves and employ "self talk." Teachers and parents should be really sensitive to signals that kids are starting to take on that role for themselves and encourage it. And if kids aren't developing self-coaching talk, then they need to be taught it.

Debriefing

Invitations to metacognitive thinking need to be sprinkled throughout the learning process, and that often requires some rethinking on the part of teachers. Not only do we typically omit the activating of prior knowledge to begin instruction, but we also don't stop frequently enough to debrief the learning process. Posing questions that help students to articulate for themselves the kinds of thinking they've been using is part of the art of reflective practice and one of the reasons why metacognitive teachers typically have smarter students.

Wonderful resources like John Barell's *Teaching for Thoughtfulness* and Bob Swartz and Sandra Parks' *Infusing the Teaching of Critical and Creative Thinking into Content Instruction* focus on developing teachers' fluency and precision in asking questions. They also demonstrate the use of co-operative learning structures that provide frequent opportunities throughout a lesson for students to stop and think about their thinking. Research cited by Jeanne Gibbs in her *Tribes: A New Way of Learning and Being Together* confirms that these "pauses to refresh" can actually double the retention of facts and concepts in an academic lesson.

Reflective questions posed during the learning process prompt students to think not only about what they are thinking but also about how they are doing it.

- What am I trying to do?
- What will it look (sound, taste, feel, smell) like when I'm finished?
- How is this similar to something I've done before? What is different?
- What are the steps in the process?
- What have I already accomplished?
- Do I need to go back and check something I did previously?
- What do I do next?

Timing is also crucial. Sometimes when we've been deeply engrossed in a thinking task, we're hard pressed to explain how we were thinking even a minute after completing the process. "Catch them thinking" is a good motto for teachers. I often notice in a classroom that when a student has an *AHA!* insight, he or she telegraphs that message through dramatic body language. I've seen kids and adults almost knocked off their chairs when a brilliant thought surfaced. That's when they need to stop and think *immediately* about what they were just thinking and how that startling connection was made. Using student observers or videotaping classroom activities can also help in capturing some of the great thinking that may otherwise go unobserved.

Teachers who value reflection often cue themselves and their students by posting key questions on the walls of their classrooms. They are also more likely to use learning logs and process journals to accompany more traditional notebooks. Even regular notebooks can be restructured by simply drawing a line down the middle of the page so that one side has notes while the other includes the students' comments, observations or conclusions — or doodles, if they help to consolidate and personalize the learning.

Teaching for transfer

Lessons designed for metacognition also bridge to other learning contexts. Just as teachers engage students in remembering prior experience, so they involve them in predicting applications for their new understandings. Three of my favourite bridging questions couldn't be simpler: *What? So what? Now what?*

These questions invite students to:

- summarize their understanding of what they've learned;
- explore the personal significance of that understanding;
- anticipate ways of applying or extending their learning.

Another simple strategy is the KWL strategy, as shown in Figure 8. At the beginning of a lesson, students fill in the first column of the chart (Know) with all the prior information they bring to the topic under investigation. The second column (Want to know) serves for generating questions: what do they want to know more about? The final column (Learned) can be used in a couple of ways: for summarizing new learnings, or for suggesting ways of investigating the answers to those questions. Sometimes filling out that third column will also prompt a return to the first section to modify some of the concepts that were present at the beginning of the lesson. A sign of real learning!

Figure 8

WHAT WE KNOW ABOUT VIKINGS	WHAT WE WANT TO KNOW	WHAT WE'VE LEARNED
• They lived long ago. • They lived in Iceland. • They had open ships with sails and oars.	• What were their houses like? • What kind of games did they play? • Could they read and write?	• They were the first white people in North America. • They had many goods.

Homework

I know I'm in the presence of a reflective teacher when I see the kinds of homework or projects they assign. A kindergarten teacher in the elementary school where my office is located has a wonderful journal that goes home with the children, together with the class mascot, a well-worn clown. Each child has a chance to take the clown home at lunchtime and keep it for the rest of the day. Parents act as scribes to record the children's stories of what the clown experienced on its field trip to the child's home.

Reading the kids' stories as transcribed by their parents has its own charm, but what thrills me more is sensing the partnership being formed between teacher and parents in support of the children's learning. It's obvious that English isn't the first language for many of those parents (and writing not their chosen mode of communication), but it's also apparent that they've put real effort into trying to capture their children's descriptions and thoughts about the highlights of the clown's visit.

Another thoughtful teacher I know has his grade eight class prepare a weekly newsletter that goes home on Friday to the parents. As they select, write and edit articles for inclusion in the paper, the kids are determining the significance of what they've learned during the week. Whenever I hear that a teacher assigns some kind of sharing with family members of what the children have learned at school, I suspect I'm hearing about a teacher who values and promotes metacognition. When I hear they've also sent home suggestions for ways parents can reinforce and extend the lessons of the classroom, I know I'm hearing about a rare gem!

Portfolios

I mentioned earlier the potential for new insights children experience when they revisit their prior learning. Many classroom teachers facilitate that process by inviting students to create portfolios or collections of their work. To function effectively as a strategy for promoting metacognition, portfolios must be more than a storage system or a random sampling of student work, however; the students must be actively involved in selecting what work will be included, according to predetermined criteria. Selected pieces will include finished products — for example, a piece of writing that has been through the whole writing process, from brainstorming ideas through revision, editing and a final polishing to ensure technical correctness — but in-process pieces are equally important.

After making their selections, the students can complete reflection sheets for each one, indicating either the particular features of the work they want the teacher to note, or their rationale for selecting it. Older students might compare selections or include more general comments on the collection as a whole. They might point out any patterns they've noted, or areas of development or improvement over time. I also like the idea of encouraging students to use De Bono's hats, or some other symbol system (see Figure 9, for example), to indicate the different kinds of thinking they see represented in their collected work. That gets them looking beyond surface features to focus on the quality of their thinking.

Some schools include a videotape in the portfolios, so the children's class presentations and performances are also on record. Families can sign these out for the weekend, and sometimes they're chosen over the latest release from the video store. After watching the videotape together, parents and child can share their reflections on a feedback form and this, too, becomes part of the student's portfolio.

Student-led conferences

A logical extension of the use of portfolios and other types of performance-based assessments is to invite students to share their reflections on their own learning with their parents and other interested adults. Innovative classroom teachers are exploring these strategies because of their enormous potential for enhancing students' understanding, involvement and sense of self-direction. Imagine, too, how valued children feel when they enjoy their family's undivided attention as they take centre-stage to share the results of their hard work. Teachers I know who have adopted this approach for reporting to parents on their students' progress would never want to go back to sending home a report card, or even arranging a traditional parent-teacher interview, because these lack the potential for intense parent-child involvement that a student-led conference provides.

Although the teacher is present in the room as the family groups are meeting, the children are in charge. They take their preparation for these conferences very seriously and are usually more than ready to

Figure 9

R — Recalling or remembering what happened.

Stating an idea and then giving an example of it.

Giving an example and then stating what it is an example of.

Giving causes and effects for what happens

Showing similarities between things.

Showing differences between things.

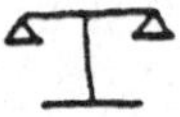
Making judgments or evaluating.

→ Predicting.

Making inferences.

id — Using personal identification.

|| — Using an analogy.

¿ — Using problem solving.

M — Metacognition, writing about your own thinking or reading.

a — Analyzing author's techniques.

(From "*Reading Workshop: Reading, Writing, Thinking*" by Sharon Kletzien and Barbara Conway Hushion.)

present their work to and answer questions from their parents. I'm always impressed by their honesty and frankness in assessing the quality of their work. The process clearly keeps the focus of assessment where it belongs, on the individual child; and it keeps the purpose of assessment — to enhance learning — in the forefront of everyone's mind.

How parents can enhance metacognition

Attending a student-led conference may happen at best a couple of times a year, but to help develop smarter kids, parents must assume the role of audience and empathetic listener on a daily basis. Last year our board ran its second weekend conference for parents and community members. When the registration form went out, the session I was offering, called "How to help your kids be smarter," filled up immediately. On the day of the conference it was standing-room only.

It's clear to me, from this and many other presentations I've made to various parent-support groups, that parents are committed to helping their children be more successful in school and are looking for expert advice to ensure that success. But most, I think, are relieved when I ask them to do one thing and one thing only: spend five minutes a day talking to their kids about what they've learned.

Learning by talking

I first heard that advice years ago in a thinking-skills workshop by an American teacher named Joyce Juntune, and everything I've read since then about the role conversation and storytelling play in enhancing memory confirms that what we share with others is what we remember. As kids retell the events of the day — what story the teacher read to the class, who they played with at recess, what they talked about over the lunch table, what happened at band practice or on the basketball court, what's being planned for the field trip — they are making connections to these events, attributing significance to those that have particular meaning for them, creating a context that will make it easier for them to recall and use the information later.

This summer I worked with a group of students who had been unsuccessful in fulfilling the requirements for their English program during the school year. Whether they were retelling a story we had read together or imagining a story about themselves that might appear in the newspaper a few years down the road, most were hard pressed to elaborate. And it wasn't only storytelling ability they lacked; several of their teachers had commented on their lack of general knowledge.

When I think about those kids, I'm reminded of a young woman I taught a number of years ago who had returned to school after dropping out at a young age. She was incredibly hardworking, persistent and highly motivated to do whatever was required and, as a result, she did well on class assignments. When she was ready to begin making the transition back to employment, she selected a co-operative education secretarial program that included a 10-week job placement.

After several weeks she came to see me quite upset. Not about her performance on the job. Her supervisor was quite satisfied with her work. Where she felt she was failing was in the part of the job that most of us take for granted: coffee break. When her fellow employees got together in the cafeteria she couldn't follow their conversations. They talked about events and places and people she knew nothing about. She had nothing to contribute to their chat.

I commented on her intelligence in identifying the problem and suggested a personal learning project: skimming the paper and news magazines on a regular basis, keeping a list of unfamiliar places and people and then hitting the library reference section periodically to check on them. She might also paraphrase what the others shared and ask follow-up questions as her part of the conversation. I could give her these few survival skills so she would feel more comfortable, but at heart I felt sad for her. As I do for the kids who don't have many dinner-table conversations about school, talk that would help them to consolidate and expand their learning.

In contrast, I remember a delightful kid who was part of an informal research study I did with a friend as part of a reading course we were taking together. We decided to investigate the reading habits of some of the students in grade nine at the school where I was librarian. The kids we interviewed made it very clear to us (especially the boys!) that personal reading wasn't a priority for them. Given the choice, they'd much rather hang out with their friends, talk on the phone or hit the nearest video arcade.

However, one of the boys was the exception. He was obviously popular with the other kids, an excellent hockey player who often spent long hours travelling to various tournaments with his team. And he was never without a book. Stephen King was his favourite author at the time and he had read all of his books. When we asked him to speculate why he was so different from the other kids in his enthusiasm for reading, he immediately had an answer: Mom. She couldn't wait to hear him talk about what he'd read, and she'd follow up on his recommendations. He didn't mind sharing this with the other kids either; he knew he had a good thing going!

That kid was a real source of inspiration for me. As a result of our study, we worked with the other teachers to think of new ways to include supplementary reading in their programs. The history teacher decided to incorporate some short fictional works into a unit on the Holocaust. One of the books he included was Elie Weisl's classic *Night*, which tells the harrowing story of a father and son being transported by train to a concentration camp. Word began to spread among the boys that this was a book worth reading. They pressured each other to read faster because others were waiting for their chance at the book. Boys would stop me in the hall for a whispered confession that they had been up until two or three o'clock and that they'd cried when they finished reading — something I wasn't to tell anyone else, of course! Which book should they read next?

I hadn't thought about that experience for a number of years, but by chance one of the teachers at summer school this year had also been on staff at that other school. Coming in from the parking lot one morning she reminded me about those kids. She also told me that when Elie Weisl won the Nobel Prize for literature a few years ago she wrote him a letter to tell him about the reaction of those students when they read *Night*.

I went into the classroom that day even more convinced that kids have to be talking about what they're learning — with each other, with their teachers, with other adults and, most of all, with their parents. That's what keeps the joy in learning.

The home gallery

Many of the metacognitive strategies teachers use have their counterparts at home. I have an artist friend who has fabulous scrapbooks of her three daughters' artwork, a home equivalent of school portfolios. Scrapbooks offer opportunities for children not only to select the work they want to save, but also to include commentaries, both when they fill their scrapbooks and when they revisit them over the years. Other parents use videotapes in much the same way teachers do, keeping an ongoing record not only of the school events they attend but also of other activities they think their kids might like to revisit periodically, to see their progress.

A childhood friend of mine who teaches grade one provides a picture frame for each child in her classroom. When the children decide it's time to change their art display, they initiate a conference with her to explain why they prefer their new selection. That's a technique that works equally well at home, whether the kids have their own picture gallery or just want to replace the current refrigerator artwork.

From learner to teacher

As a parent I was delighted to receive a newsletter from the principal of my son's school that cited research on the power of various strategies in helping children to learn and retain new information. There's a sliding scale that goes from low to high:

I hear	I see	I see and hear someone do	I discuss with others	I experience personally	I teach others
14%	22%	30%	42%	83%	91%

Inviting children to teach what they've learned to peers or younger children is a powerful metacognitive strategy parents can employ.

I'm sure I'm not the only first-born child whose younger sibling could already read before going to school — I couldn't wait to get home and get out my chalkboard and chalk and teach her what I had learned in school that day! My son doesn't have a younger sibling, but I enjoy hearing him describe the strategies he's using as a reading buddy for a grade one child this year. His buddy tends to guess at words based on their initial letter, and Christian has developed a range of helpful techniques that would do a reading teacher proud.

And there are lots of times when kids can act as mentors for their parents as well. I have more trouble programming a VCR than the average five-year-old does, and I'm sure I'm not alone in that. Kids can not only *do* that kind of thing easily, but also explain so we can understand!

SUMMARY

Metacognition is one characteristic of smart people. AHA! moments happen regularly if we give children opportunities to revisit previous learning experiences and talk about how their understanding has changed over time. Unfortunately, this kind of reflective thinking isn't common, even in adults. As parents and teachers, we need to encourage kids to think about how they take in, sort and "file" information.

CHAPTER 9

JUDGING ONE'S WORTH

In a *Newsweek* article Robert Fulghum, author of *Everything I Ever Wanted to Know I Learned in Kindergarten*, talks about the different reactions he typically gets when he goes into a kindergarten class and a first-year university class. He often asks students to raise their hands if they sing, dance, paint, write stories, etc. In the kindergarten class everyone is a singer, dancer, artist, author or anything else he might suggest; but by late adolescence only a few students identify themselves as any of those people. Some may admit to belting out Broadway tunes in the shower or dancing under the influence, but most have a whole list of things they don't do. Why? What happens between the ages of five and 18?

Two workplace models

One day as I was thumbing through two very different business books, I noticed that both contained a chapter on employee reviews by supervisors. Intrigued, I read those two chapters, jotting down notes as I read. Then I reorganized the information using a compare/contrast chart. What I saw emerging, as shown in Figure 11, were two very different models for evaluation.

Which model looks more familiar when you think about your own experiences on the job? Is someone responsible for assessing your job performance periodically and then sitting down with you to review that assessment? Or are you an equal partner in the assessment process, helping to establish performance targets, monitoring your own performance and providing your supervisor with data that shows you're on track? Can you ask for feedback whenever it would be helpful, or do you have to wait for review time to find out how you're doing? Are all the criteria you're being evaluated by clear to you? Do you have access to all the information gathered in assessing your performance?

I live in an interesting assessment world. My performance is offi-

Figure 11

MODEL A	COMPARED TO IN TERMS OF	MODEL B
1. Standards are uniform for all.	STANDARDS	Standards differ for each individual.
2. Performance criteria are predetermined by the evaluator.	CRITERIA	Performance criteria are negotiated by boss and employee.
3. Evaluation intervals are preset (e.g., annual review).	TIMING	Evaluation is ongoing.
4. Feedback is very general ("an asset to the company").	SPECIFICITY	Feedback is tailored to the employee.
5. Evaluation is closely tied to rewards/punishments (e.g., pay raise, promotion).	CONSEQUENCES	Assessment and rewards are kept separate.
6. Delay is common between action and feedback.	TIMELINESS	Feedback is closely timed to action.
7. Responsibility is top down.	RESPONSIBILITY	Responsibility is lateral.
8. Comments are summative ("another good year for the sales division").	USE OF FEEDBACK	Comments are formative (include suggestions for improvement/personal growth plan).
9. Employee may comment after the fact (box at bottom of form for response).	EMPLOYEE FEEDBACK	Employee may share in writing of evaluation report.
10. Accountability is the bottom line.	UNDERLYING PURPOSE OF ASSESSMENT	Supports professional growth and development.

cially evaluated every three years, and the assessment document is part of my permanent file as an employee of the board of education. The criteria for what constitutes competency as a teacher are fairly common: effective classroom management is usually high on the list; for secondary teachers, knowledge of one's subject area probably comes second; the ability to plan and deliver instruction that keeps the kids reasonably alert is important; participation in the life of the school is often included, although here expectations seem to change as teachers get older.

Between reviews, however, I'm often left without either Model A or Model B in place, the expectation being that I will monitor my own performance and work competently without direct supervision. If I want more feedback about how I'm doing, I have to take the initiative to elicit a more specific response. For me, that usually means asking workshop participants to complete a questionnaire evaluating the usefulness of what I've presented and inviting suggestions for ways of improving it. I use that feedback to determine what I might do to improve my effectiveness as a staff-development trainer.

What lies at the heart of each model?

The book I developed Model A from was written for bosses by a former aide to Ronald Reagan. Its title? *How to Fire an Employee*. Its author assumes that every employee is a potential "firee," so he's advising employers to follow a cover-your-butt approach. If you're going to be hauled into court for wrongful dismissal, it helps if you can convince the judge that the rules were the same for everyone and that all the procedures were followed rigorously. So it's basically an accountability model. The process tries to keep everyone in line by using performance review as a carrot-and-stick motivation. It doesn't have much to do with developing the potential of the individual employee.

Model B came from a chapter on coaching as a way of enhancing employee performance in a collection of essays called *Motivation of Personnel*. Its author assumes a commitment between employer and employee based on the employer's assumption that the worker wants to do a good job. Employer and worker negotiate a review process that allows each partner to make continuous improvement in developing the skills, knowledge and attitudes that underlie expert performance. This model assumes that each individual is the final arbiter of the quality of his or her performance. Eventually the coach has to retreat to the sidelines and let the player get on with the game. At that point the coach gets feedback about his or her effectiveness as well, from the player's ability to take the coaching suggestions and put them into play. It's a symbiotic relationship in which two partners share the gains and losses.

At the heart of both models is one fundamental question: who is responsible for judging one's work? Model A comes down clearly in favour of external evaluation, while Model B opts for internal assessment. Art Costa, one of my favourite authors on thinking, is a definite Model B theorist. He maintains that teaching students to be self-assessing should be the ultimate goal of any form of assessment adults use with them.

Assessment expert Richard Stiggins also talks about helping students to become "informed consumers" of evaluative feedback. Otherwise they are faced with two equally unappealing choices: to be totally dependent upon outside assessment and reinforcement, or to set up elaborate mechanisms for filtering evaluative feedback so they have to deal with only the good news. Either way, they aren't internalizing objective criteria that would allow them to take more responsibility for setting, monitoring and evaluating their own learning goals.

Evaluation at school

Most kids' natural self-confidence and enthusiasm for learning are still high when they enter school, so what is it that happens in school? Let's look first at the results of such assessment issues as feedback, motivation, competence and self-esteem.

Carrots and sticks

I once read about a study conducted with young children in a daycare centre that really made me think about the connections among those four assessment issues. A group of researchers randomly assigned the children to one of three groups. Then they videotaped them for two weeks at the centre's painting corner. They timed how long each child spent at the painting centre and had art experts assess the quality of the childrens' painting, focusing particularly on their originality.

Then they began a two-week intervention. Spending time in the painting corner was positively reinforced for children in the first group. For example, they were given access to Polaroid cameras so they could take their own pictures, a privilege that was highly valued by the kids. Children in the second group were subjected to art criticism, having to justify why their sun was painted something other than yellow or why their bird didn't look much like a bird. The kids assigned to the control group were left alone to paint what and as much as they liked, without comment.

When the two weeks were over, the researchers went back to videotaping and assessing the children's artwork. At this point I often ask my students to predict what changes, if any, the researchers observed in the children's art and in the amount of time they chose to spend in the painting centre. Most predict correctly that the kids who were negatively reinforced avoided the painting corner like the plague and that the behaviour of the children in the control group didn't change. Most also assume that the kids who were reinforced with the Polaroid camera spent lots more time painting and, since they had more practice, produced better paintings.

Wrong! Once the kids twigged to the fact that they were no longer going to be rewarded for painting, they didn't see much reason to persist with the activity, so they actually spent less time painting than they'd spent initially. Moreover, the quality of the art they produced during the two weeks when they were being presented with "carrots" was deemed by the art experts to be less original than their previous painting.

So what happened? Well, apparently children are much like adults in their jobs. When they feel they have relative autonomy over how they pursue their work, and when the impact of external rewards doesn't overwhelm their internal motivation to do a competent job, they actually work harder and produce better quality results. The same factors that contribute to employee satisfaction or dissatisfaction are at work in the daycare centre, the classroom and the home. It seems to be human nature that, while we're willing to accept direction about what we have to do, when an authority figure tries to direct how we are to work, either by mandating the process or by trying to shape our behaviour through rewards and punishments, then we get our backs up and our work suffers as a result.

Competence and self-esteem

Young children seem to be particularly good at setting themselves reasonable standards when they are first trying to learn a new skill. For example, beginning readers don't expect to be as proficient as older children, so they tend to measure their progress by how far they've come and how much effort they're putting into mastering the new task. When they encounter children of their own age who already know how to read, they use that information to set future expectations for themselves and observe these children to try to help their own learning.

In *Competence Considered,* Sternberg cites studies that suggest young children "have high self-perceptions of competence and expectations for success and seem to be resilient to failure." (p. 169) However, once kids start basing their self-perceptions on negative comparisons with other children, their estimation of their own competence begins to slip.

This point is very nicely made in a paperback for beginning readers called *First Grade Takes a Test,* a book I think should be required reading for all teachers and parents, let alone kids! In the story, first grade is humming along quite nicely until some unidentified authority arrives to administer a standardized test to the kids. The author, Miriam Cohen, does a really nice job of suggesting how ludicrous some test items can be when they don't match the kids' experience.

For example, the children are asked to choose among three things to determine what firemen do: make bread, put out fires, sing. Poor Sammy has trouble with this one because his only direct experience with firemen was their arrival to help his uncle get his head out of a pipe he got stuck in, and that's not one of the options. Jim has problems with a question designed to check his concept of relative size and his understanding of comparative adjectives, because he gets hung up on the picture. He's more interested in whether it's really a baloney sandwich the girl is handing to the boy and can't understand what tallness has to do with the picture.

You get the point: first grade is going down in flames. Except for Anna Maria, the embodiment of school smarts.

The story also reinforces the importance of time in giving feedback since, by the time the mysterious lady returns with the test scores, the kids have all forgotten the test. Nevertheless, the results are there. Anna Maria is hauled off to the class for the gifted down the hall and the rest of the kids begin to call each other dummies. One child even starts whispering the epithet to himself.

Things are looking pretty grim for the kids, self-esteem wise, until their own teacher intercedes and gets them back on track with a passionate speech on all the qualities that can't be measured by a test. "You can build things! You can read books! You can make pictures! The test doesn't tell you if you are a kind person who helps your friend. Those are important things." Her indictment of standardized tests, along with a round of homemade cookies, saves the day.

The story ends happily when Anna Maria wisely rejects the offer of special status and returns to take her rightful place as mentor to the rest of grade one. Since kids easily get the point of this story, it can lead to interesting discussions on a number of levels about the assumptions that underlie some testing practices.

Judging by comparison

Later in the learning process, when the basics have been acquired, comparisons may be useful in helping children to assess their abilities and to think about future choices. Interestingly, kids who are having difficulty mastering new skills may cling more tenaciously to comparisons with their peer group in judging their own skill level than those who are more sure of their competence.

It would seem more logical for higher performing kids to bolster their sense of mastery by comparing their achievements with students who are less skilled, but it seems that a belief in our competence frees us in some way from the need for outside confirmation of our own perceptions. On the other hand, children who are less certain of their competence are more likely to be affected by both positive and negative feedback. As children get older, many find ways of avoiding comparisons in order to salvage their fragile egos.

What research is suggesting is that, at different times in our lives and at different stages of mastering new skills, we need the flexibility, as learners, to shift our perspective and modify the standards by which we judge our own performance. Otherwise we may grow discouraged and give up on tasks that, with more persistence, we might eventually master. Or we may begin to define ourselves as incapable.

The onset of that self-limiting process seems to coincide with beginning school, and I can't help but wonder what the connection might be between lower self-perceptions of competence and the opportunities that school provides for making unflattering comparisons between oneself and one's peers. When kids begin to define "smart" as meaning "doing better than others," their goal often becomes establishing superiority over their peers. Then learning becomes a means to an end rather than an end in itself and, over time, this perspective contributes to a decline in enthusiasm for learning.

Without this kind of comparison kids are more likely to learn from the example of more competent peers without themselves feeling incompetent. They can focus on the task at hand rather than devoting a lot of their energy to maintaining their status within the group. Adolescents who are focused on the task of learning rather than on trying to outdo their peers tend to define the goal of school as helping them to prepare to be responsible, constructive members of society. Teens oriented to competing with their peers are more likely to see school as helping to prepare them to achieve wealth and social status.

The illusion of incompetence

Even among the most able children, there are no guarantees that they will see themselves as competent. Research suggests that the "illusion of incompetence" emerges early in elementary school, leaving kids with:

- low expectations of success;
- a belief that their parents and teachers see them as "unable";
- a reluctance to try, or to persist with, challenging tasks;
- anxiety about evaluation;
- self-criticism.

When kids lose the developmental perspective on their learning, which allowed them to explain away their lack of competence as a temporary aberration that a few years would correct, the prospect of failure and the resulting feeling of incompetence become more threatening. Once children cotton on to the idea that ability is a limiting factor, they begin to devalue and avoid those activities they don't feel confident in, although they might once have enjoyed them.

Researchers cite children's participation in voluntary sports activities as a good example of this trend: when children begin to differentiate between effort and ability, they also begin to withdraw from sports. Instead, they tend to seek membership in a peer group whose members share a common disdain for a particular activity — not a great prospect if the activity being disdained is school!

Most adults, if we're working on tasks we find inherently interesting or enjoyable, don't spend time worrying about our ability; we find satisfaction in exercising our skills, attaining new understanding or performing more efficiently. But even adults can be forced out of this self-accepting mindset into an anxious concern about our ability by one or more of the external factors typically found in schools:

- tests;
- evaluative comments that focus attention on our level of competence;
- a climate that promotes competition with others.

In other words, *grades* and *praise*!

Evaluation at home

Now let's put on a different hat and think about which of the two models described earlier fits most closely with our practice as parents.

- If you have more than one child, do you have consistent standards for what constitutes acceptable behaviour? Or do you vary your expectations to suit the age, gender, personalities, etc. of your children?
- Are the criteria by which you judge their performance clear to them? For example, if the kids are entertaining friends are they sure what they can and can't do without losing the privilege of inviting a buddy home? Or do the rules depend on who the friend is and what kind of a day you're having?

- Are the kids involved in setting family expectations? Or do they simply follow the rules of the house?
- Do they have to wait for the reviews? ("Just wait until your father gets home!") Or is feedback instantaneous?
- Is there room for growth? ("Next time I'd prefer that you ask me ahead of time rather than inviting your friend to stay for dinner and putting me on the spot by asking if it's O.K.") Or is the assessment pretty final? ("That's the last time you'll be allowed to have a friend stay for dinner.")
- Are there obvious rewards for complying with the standards? ("That's a great report card. We'll treat you to pizza and a video — and no dishes for tonight.") Are there punishments for deviating from the rules? ("Don't even bother asking me if you can go to the dance on Friday, missie, not after what you just did!")

Which model do you see yourself leaning toward in your evaluator role? Or do you often have a foot in each? If so, you may be causing problems for your kids because you're giving them some very strange messages.

Parental expectations

Research suggests that parents have a major influence on children's perceptions of their ability. As a matter of fact, in a study described in *Competence Considered* (p.53), parents' perceptions proved to be a more powerful predictor of children's self-perceptions than grades or test scores. Girls tended to perceive their mothers in particular as having lower expectations for them. And mothers often do set lower academic standards for a daughter than for a son, even when actual achievements indicate the same level of competence. This pattern is particularly common in the area of math.

Parents of daughters should be especially concerned because research also suggests that as girls get older they are increasingly likely to underestimate their abilities. A follow-up study of grade nine students who had originally been studied in grade five showed that, in the later study, girls comprised 100% of the group who underestimated their actual level of ability.

Also, as children approach adolescence, their ability to meet parental demands becomes a matter of particular concern. When kids get the message that they're letting their parents down, they become caught in a self-perpetuating negative feedback loop. At the extreme, a feeling of hopelessness about ever being able to meet their parents' expectations — and fear that their parents' support depends on that — is a contributing factor in teenage suicide.

What's the alternative?

There are clear options for both teachers and parents. Even though most education systems are still firmly into evaluating by external standards, end-of-unit tests and standardized examinations, individual teachers can define themselves as on a continuum between the two models and try to incorporate evaluation practices that are more in keeping with the coaching model. These would include involving students in:

- developing the criteria and standards for assessing their work;
- selecting assignments for assessment from a collected body of work;
- determining alternative ways of demonstrating mastery of content and skills;
- self-assessing;
- providing feedback to other students;
- selecting exemplary work to serve as models for other students;
- reporting progress to parents.

In his book *Punished by Rewards*, Alfie Kohn also suggests that teachers:

- use oral or written comments instead of grades on most assignments;
- indicate that work of poor quality is incomplete;
- ask students if they are ready for evaluation rather than forcing them into a situation of trying to demonstrate competence when they're not prepared (no more pop quizzes, thanks!);
- assess achievement, not effort;
- avoid anything that looks even remotely like a bell curve!

My experience in the classroom supports Kohn's suggestion that we should talk about assessment with our students. I found years ago that when I asked students to brainstorm the functions of assessment for the various audiences who received feedback collected through tests and assignments (including students, teachers, parents, employers, admissions boards, etc.), they never included more informed decision-making as one of the chief reasons why those parties would want to collect data on student progress in a systematic way. They didn't seem to realize that teachers need feedback in order to assess the effectiveness of their instruction and plan for the next stage.

From their perspective, assessment was nothing more than a carrot-and-stick motivator: either rewarding achievement or punishing lack of effort. Many students also considered grades intrinsically motivating. That's when I would usually tell my story about the kids in the painting centre. Students need to put assessment into a larger context, as just one part of an ongoing decision-making process, if grades aren't to become an end unto themselves.

At the same time, I was up front about the dilemma I found myself in as their teacher. I pointed out that, while I preferred to work with them in the Model B style, I was periodically required to report on their progress using Model A criteria. I explained that having a foot in each model was going to create some discontinuity, especially when the school ground to a halt for examinations every three months. However, we would work together to keep those assessments in their proper place as just one way of collecting data. I also designed the mandated assessments so they were as close to standard practice in the classroom as possible. No multiple-choice quizzes, for example, when a videotaped group problem-solving activity would provide better evidence of their knowledge or mastery of particular skills.

I also delayed assessment until I was confident that the students had internalized the standards for a competent performance; there's no sense testing students on something if they don't know what it looks, sounds and feels like when it's done well. And I made sure that self-assessment was built into the process. It's become fairly standard practice these days for teachers to provide a feedback form (a checklist or reflection sheet, for example) that students complete and submit along with their completed projects. When students have predicted how they will score on each of the assessment criteria, the feedback they receive from the assessor becomes much more meaningful. Either their own assessment is validated as accurate (always nice to know that you were on target!) or they get strong disconfirming feedback that should set off alarm bells.

Either way, they are much less likely to do what I often saw in my early years in the classroom. Surely I'm not the only teacher who has spent hours putting comments on essays or tests only to have the students flip immediately to the final page to check out the grade. Then they would either gloat to their less fortunate peers or do the famous crumple-and-heave routine, with the offending document landing in the nearest trash can!

Preparing students for tests and examinations

When I'm using paper-and-pencil testing as an evaluation tool, I still want students involved in monitoring and assessing their performance. To do that, I first have to teach test-taking skills explicitly. (See also the mindmapping technique, page 90.) Fortunately there are excellent resource materials for both teachers and students that demystify the process of taking tests. Some of the strategies students need to practise include:

Gathering information about the format of the test

They need to know the types of questions there'll be, what course content is included, the length of time they'll have, how the answers will be marked, etc. When I worked with adult students, I was amazed to discover that many of them thought that asking the instructor questions about the test was cheating! I explained that they needed this information in order to know how best to prepare; you study very differently if you're going to be responding to multiple-choice questions than if you'll be writing essay answers.

Using effective techniques for review

When I worked with high school students I found that most of them had one strategy for review: reading their notes over and over again. Research shows that repetition is one of the least effective (and most inefficient) strategies for committing facts to memory. And material learned this way is likely to fly right out the classroom window should the deadly test-anxiety bug take hold.

Much better for students to generate possible test questions, either on their own or with classmates. These will help them to focus their review and, even if they're not very good at predicting the actual questions on the test, the fact that they are reviewing their notes with that purpose in mind will make their study more focused and productive. And predicting fairly accurately often isn't too difficult.

A colleague of mine was sitting in on a lecture with a group of college students just before their midterm exam. What was evident to her as a teacher — that the instructor was using this final class to give the students all kinds of hints about what was going to be on the exam — went right over the heads of many of the students. They weren't attuned to the cues: "This is important." "This would make a good test question." "This bears repeating." Many of them were so worried about the test that they had already stopped listening — or had even skipped the last class so they'd have more time to study!

Surveying the test and planning strategy

This I found was the toughest nut to crack. When students receive their test papers the temptation to read the first question and start writing is often overwhelming, especially if everyone around you launches in with the same fever pitch. However, a few minutes spent reading through the questions first, checking the marking scheme, allocating time to each question depending on its mark, and planning the sequence in which to answer the questions — these strategies can make all the difference to a student's achievement.

This was brought home to me when I worked with a young woman who had been refused admission to a nursing program because she failed a standardized literacy test, a prerequisite for admission. Not realizing that she would be penalized for every incomplete answer, she had worked slowly and methodically through each question. What she completed was probably quite good; however, once the examiners deducted the marks for every question she didn't get to, her score was in the failing range.

We practised taking this type of test, paying particular attention to the need to monitor time. She worked through several sample tests, quickly completing the answers she knew most readily and then going back to tackle the harder ones, leaving those she was most unsure of to the very end. We also boned up on some specific strategies for dealing with the multiple-choice format.

When next she took the test, she scored in the 98th percentile. Had her literacy skills improved that much in a few months? Not really. They were probably okay to begin with. Learning to control her test anxiety by preparing carefully, planning her strategy and monitoring her performance throughout the test made the difference.

Reviewing the test and making necessary revisions

Once I had taught the test-taking strategies, whenever we had a test there were two evaluations occurring simultaneously. While I was gathering data about the students' mastery of course content, they were gathering information about their test-taking skills. I allocated time at the end of the test for them to go back over their papers and comment on their process while it was fresh in their minds. Through observation, I could also share data with them; for example, I could monitor how much time individuals spent in planning before they began answering questions. Finally, they used the marking scheme to predict their mark on each test item and total their final score.

Returning their test papers gave me another opportunity to debrief the process, using the additional information provided by my comments and marks. If particular questions had proved difficult for a number of students in the class, we would analyze those in more detail to try to determine why. The students could also share their strategies. Although we were working in some ways in Model A, I was trying to build in as much self- and peer-coaching as possible.

A by-product

While the benefits to students of using assessment to enhance learning is, I hope, becoming clear, I must also mention an interesting consequence for me. As Richard Stiggins points out quite clearly in his research, most classroom teachers have had very little formal training in effective assessment procedures, either in their initial preparation for teaching or through inservicing. That was certainly true in my case.

However, what I have found is that, as I've worked with my students to help them understand the role of evaluation in the learning process, my own interest and proficiency in assessment have been enhanced. For example, if I'm using a test not only to confirm my students' understanding of course content but also to teach them the more general skills of test-taking, I'm much more thoughtful about both the structure and the content of the test. I'm getting smarter about testing and I know that benefits us all.

The final seal of approval

I can be doing all sorts of wonderful Model B coaching and assessment in the classroom but, as a teacher, I must remember what the research confirms: for most students, it's still their parents who will put the final seal of approval on what happens at school. At school the mark-book may reign supreme. At home the fridge test rules. What goes up there is what the child ultimately sees as valued. What goes into a scrapbook or file, what gets mentioned on the phone to Grandma or bragged about at a dinner party, that's what kids are going to remember.

That's a compelling reason for teachers and parents to share the same kind of informed discourse about assessment that I described earlier when talking about teachers and students. If we're approaching the kids from opposite perspectives — if I'm talking continuous progress and the parents are asking where the child stands in relation to the kid down the street; if the parents are promoting doing a good job as its own reward and I'm busy stamping the kids' work with happy faces — then we need to begin to work together to find some common ground.

SUMMARY

Children learn better if they believe in their own competence, have some autonomy in how they learn, and aren't pressured by external rewards and expectations. If self-assessment is our goal for them, we must begin to bring our children into the assessment process and make them the final judge of their own performance.

CHAPTER 10

SOLVING LIFE'S PROBLEMS

Even if we all share the same goal — to teach people to think better, whether those people are six or 60 — we won't find the task an easy one. Life is just too messy and unpredictable. How can you practise effective problem-solving if you don't even know you have a problem until it's almost too late to do something about it? Real-life problems often forget to announce themselves as problems; they come in various guises, like a party for a bunch of rambunctious six-year-olds, or a strange new engine knock, or even an unexpected lottery win. Being able to recognize that a situation requires problem-solving is sometimes the real problem!

If we want to give students opportunities to practise thinking skills in ways that aren't irrelevant or artificial, we have to provide real, meaningful problems that include a chance for them to put their decision-making and action-planning into effect, so they can see the results. For example, Skills for Action, a secondary school program from Lions-Quest, uses problem-solving to teach personal and social responsibility. After taking students step by step through the process of conducting a needs assessment for their community, it invites them to determine whether they should complete a volunteer placement with a local agency or work together to develop their own response to an assessed need. This might take the form of an advocacy campaign to raise awareness of the need, or of a service project — perhaps a clothing drive, or the establishment of an after-school homework club for the neighbourhood children.

Howard Gardner makes an interesting suggestion in *The Unschooled Mind*. He thinks that schools should take another look at the concept of apprenticeship. Historically, this was the normal avenue for many young people to make the transition to employment and full participation in the life of the community. Mentorship by an experienced adult and the acquisition of knowledge and skills through doing are both powerful learning strategies, but how many young people today can pursue those options?

Professional training usually incorporates some aspect of apprenticeship, but why should students have to wait until adulthood to work alongside reflective practitioners who can help them to critique their own learning? Gardner's book includes examples of schools that are trying to break down the old model of the solitary teacher working alone with a classroom full of kids. These schools are inviting other adults to take a more active role in the children's learning and finding ways of giving the kids access to more learning opportunities beyond the classroom.

I remember hearing years ago about a group of grade three students who got excited about taxidermy after a visit by a local retiree. These children set up their own natural history museum in the classroom, using road-kill animals donated by the highway department. A taxidermist did the stuffing, and the kids designed dioramas that pictured the animals in their natural habitat. Then they acted as tour guides for younger students who came to visit their museum.

Choices for children

One way to elicit more real-life thinking from children is to present them with significant choices. It's a concept we often pay lip-service to, but sometimes it's just the illusion of choice we're providing.

Choices at school

This is especially true when it comes to decisions in the classroom. Who determines the curriculum? The instructional strategies? The assessment? The members of small groups? The arrangement of the furniture?

That last one hit me one day when my son, in grade two, arrived home highly indignant. The day after their regular teacher left on maternity leave, the kids arrived in class to find not only a new teacher but the entire room rearranged! When they protested, the new teacher explained that it was her prerogative to arrange the room in a way that met her needs — but if my child was typical, the class wasn't buying it.

She was just doing what most teachers do, however. We arrive in the classroom the week before school opens and organize things to suit our preferences. And sometimes we forget we're not the only ones who have to live with our decisions. As a child myself, whether the teacher would seat the class in alphabetical order or let us choose our own desk used to make or break the school year for me. I hated classes where I got stuck in the back of the centre row because my last name fell in the middle of the alphabet! I felt out of the action and definitely too far away from my best friend, whose initials put her right up front.

When it comes to curriculum decisions, there's even less hope that kids' preferences will be the focal point of discussion. I've sat through many a course review and planning session, and I can't remember many that started off with "I wonder what the kids would like to learn this year?" Nor have I experienced a school year that ends with the current crop of kids helping to redesign the program based on their recent experiences. Occasionally we ask the kids for feedback on the materials or the projects, but how committed are we to actually using their suggestions?

When I asked my son, just before he began grade five, what he was hoping to learn that year, chemistry and nuclear fission were two topics he thought might be neat. I suspected he was in for a disappointment! But a growing body of research suggests that, when kids have some autonomy in choosing what they learn and how they learn it, they use those options well. They:

- complete more work in less time;
- produce higher-quality, more creative work;
- are more motivated to persist with tasks, even those that aren't initially interesting;
- demonstrate higher-level reasoning;
- select tasks that are at the appropriate level of challenge.

So why not nuclear fission in grade five? The great educational theorist Jerome Bruner maintains that "any subject can be taught effectively in some intellectually honest form to any child at any stage of development." (p.5) Training teachers in instructional strategies that promote student autonomy is the key. As they become more comfortable with those strategies, they may find that the goal of providing some discretionary time each day for students to pursue their particular intellectual interests can be accommodated.

Choices at home

The same is true at home. A few years ago when I asked a group of classroom teachers to identify issues that created conflict between teachers and parents, one group mentioned homework. The teachers were trying to promote a daily homework policy; the parents were protesting because their children were already actively involved in sports teams, music and dance classes, youth and church organizations. Both groups were sure that their priorities were the most significant. A thought crossed my mind: where did the kids fit into this discussion? Was there any room for *their* priorities or even for flexibility in addressing the needs of individual children?

As adults, we have options we're not always ready to extend to kids. I'd hate for you to see the number of half-completed craft projects I have stored in my den, for example. Somehow the penguin sweater I enthusiastically started in November seemed a less compelling project when I still didn't have the back done by April. Because I'm not a seasoned knitter, I frequently choose patterns that are too complex; I've got myself (and my yarn) tied into knots on more than one occasion trying to juggle three or four colours in a design. So the project goes into a bag at the back of a cupboard. But do I have to justify the upfront cost for materials or the hours of time I spent with nothing to show? Only to myself.

When we got a brochure announcing that Saturday morning heritage language classes would be available in our area, I explained to my son, who was interested in learning another language besides French, that the classes were primarily designed for children whose families spoke a first language other than English, but that if he was interested he could probably attend. He decided to give Russian a try. The teacher was willing to accommodate him in the class but, since he was the only non-native speaker, he would have to work on his own a good deal of the time. We invested in a pocket tape-recorder and a beginner's dictionary/workbook to supplement the materials the teacher provided.

Christian was making reasonable progress at Christmas, according to the teacher's report, but in the new year his enthusiasm for getting up early on Saturdays to rush off to another class was definitely waning. To quit or not to quit, that was the question. What complicated the issue was his concern for my reaction. He'd probably overheard a few telephone conversations that sounded too much like Mom crediting her own gene pool for his emerging talent in linguistics to feel confident in saying "niet" to further Russian lessons.

After a few tears on both sides (and some reality therapy from Dad) I recognized that it wasn't really a moral issue. He opted to quit.

Negotiation skills

If we agree that in order to make kids smarter we need to give them more opportunities for problem-solving and personal decision-making, we should make sure that they have the skills necessary to be effective negotiators as well. In fact, I've found that teaching negotiation skills is one of the most realistic and readily transferable ways to promote higher-level thinking both at home and at school.

If we look at a composite picture of effective negotiators in the business world we find that, in addition to certain personality traits like patience, persistence and empathy, these people are skilled in the three kinds of thinking that people like De Bono and Sternberg label *critical, creative* and *constructive* (or practical) thinking. The three kinds of intelligence we characterized as Alice, Barbara and Celia in discussing Sternberg's triarchic model come together in the best negotiators.

Critical/analytical thinking (Alice)

One of the key factors that separates expert negotiators from the rest of us is their analytical approach to resolving conflicts. We often jump into a conflict armed with the facts as we see them and try to persuade the other party to adopt our perspective on the problem; skilled negotiators, on the other hand, assume that at best they know only half of the story. They assume that the other party's perspective is equally valid. Both parties' needs and wishes have to be clear if the end goal is to find a resolution that will be mutually satisfying.

The critical-thinking approach is especially helpful in exploring different viewpoints and clarifying the issues to be negotiated. It's also a practical application for many of the research skills we want kids to learn:

- researching background history to the conflict;
- identifying key facts;
- clarifying both what is known and what needs to be learned;
- asking questions;
- paraphrasing and summarizing main points;
- classifying the type of conflict.

But analytical fact-finding, sorting and prioritizing aren't the only skills negotiators have to practise.

Creative thinking (Barbara)

Skilled negotiators are also like the magician who seemingly pulls coins and cards out of empty air. What often turns a negotiation around is the ability to think quickly and generate options that appeal to the imagination of one or both parties. People who have the most difficulty dealing with conflict are those who can't see possibilities or choices. That may be why they lock themselves into my-way-or-the-highway, take-it-or-leave-it ultimatums, or feel the despair that accompanies their belief that they have no choices or alternatives.

Creative thinkers know from experience that first ideas aren't always the best ideas, so they build into the negotiation process lots of time for discussing alternatives. They keep a lot of balls in the air, like jugglers. They use the best thinking of both parties by bouncing the ideas of one off the other, refining their own thinking through this give and take. They keep possibilities open by suggesting options that, although seemingly impractical, contain the kernel of a workable idea.

Less skilled negotiators try to deal with each factor in the negotiation process separately, so they can cross off items on their mental checklist as they go. But in doing that, they eliminate some of the "wiggle room" they may need later.

Constructive/practical thinking (Celia)

You've done your homework like Alice. You've primed your creative pump like Barbara. Surely you're ready to take the negotiation world by storm? Wrong. The most important part of all is the awareness of context, timing and flexibility that is characteristic of a constructive intelligence.

Negotiators with this kind of smarts know there's no substitute for experience, and so they look for opportunities to hone their skills. Their motto is "There's no harm in asking" and they do. For true negotiators, the fun is the process.

Their metacognitive awareness helps in monitoring the negotiation process. Because they worked through a number of scenarios in their preplanning, they can adjust their approach if something isn't working. They're usually very clear about their non-negotiables, but they also have a flexibility that allows them to take advantage of the present reality.

Sternberg believes that's the factor that brings these people to the C.E.O.'s chair in major corporations, or to similar success in other fields. While others make do with a singular approach to dealing with situations that require negotiation, the person with practical intelligence feels comfortable with a variety of styles. They're more selective about the conflicts they engage in and quicker to cut their losses if they see a no-win situation developing. They know when to push a bit to keep discussions from bogging down, and they keep coming back to the big picture if a disagreement over details or an unwillingness to see another point of view is undermining the process.

These expert negotiators have the kind of problem-solving approach to negotiation and conflict management that makes it possible for win-win options to emerge and collaborative relationships to develop. That's what makes them a valuable asset in any culture that requires ongoing negotiations among its members or with outside partners.

Negotiating at home

If you're dealing with a toddler who has just discovered "no," debating every morning with an eight-year-old (who wants to look 14) about what to wear to school, blessed with an 11-year-old who believes that everything is negotiable, or confronted by a teenager who has only you standing between him and body piercing, then preparing kids for a C.E.O.'s chair may not be the most compelling rationale for teaching your children to negotiate. Let's think instead about how it might save some wear and tear on families!

The adolescents I work with are quick to bring up conflicts with parents. When I ask them to create imaginary situations for practising their problem-solving skills, parent-child conflicts are most commonly produced. I find teenagers enormously critical of the way parents typically deal with problems; their top complaint is that their parents refuse to listen when they try to present their perspective.

When I work with parents, however, I hear the same complaint: "My son (or daughter) won't listen to me." Neither side really understands the other's point of view, yet both wonder why nothing seems to get resolved without a lot of anger, frustration and disappointment. It's almost as if the two sides have to wear each other down before an uneasy peace can be restored.

Most negotiation models have three basic steps:

- State the problem clearly.
- Generate alternative solutions.
- Choose the best option and do it.

When I do workshops for families, I suggest that they highlight those steps on a poster, using language that's familiar to all family members and including simple illustrations or symbols that will help to personalize the steps. The poster can go on the fridge or in any other location where lots of conflicts occur. (I always enjoy listening to the discussion when family members suggest possible places — the door of the bathroom, for example, or above the TV screen, or in the front hallway where the last-minute morning rush sets off shouting matches.) It's that easy! Even preschool children can follow the steps, with assistance. Then, as the children get older and are more analytical in their thinking processes, the steps can be elaborated and refined.

Seeking to understand

Have you ever engaged in an interminable discussion with a partner and finally realized, after an hour or so, that you weren't even talking about the same problem? That's a fairly common occurrence when we make the mistake of assuming that the other person sees a situation in the same way we do.

To make this point with kids, I ask them to write a brief description of a recent problem they experienced with a parent. In no time they've got a file card filled with all the gory details. Then I ask them to turn the card over and retell the problem as they think their parent would. Getting kids to acknowledge that there might be another perspective is tough work, but I'm not convinced that, as adults, we're any more likely to remember how things look from an adolescent's perspective without the same kind of prompting.

Highly trained mediators who work in community settings to help resolve disputes between neighbours, or between citizens and officials, often find that long-standing problems can be resolved quite successfully if they can get both parties to listen to and acknowledge the other's side of the story. In his book *The 7 Habits of Highly Effective People* Stephen Covey has a wonderful chapter that describes the power of listening to understand.

When we're in conflict with a partner, what we want is to be understood. All of our energy is directed into making our argument as forcefully as possible, because we mistakenly assume that we can get our partner to change his or her mind and see the problem our way. Covey suggests that a far more effective strategy is to listen first to the other person's perspective — but not in our usual way, as if we were the D.A. gathering evidence, or the captain of a rival debating team just waiting for the speaker to finish so we can attack. Instead, we need to listen openly, with an honest desire to experience the problem as it's being described by our partner.

That's a strategy I recommend to kids: if Mom or Dad is angry with you, listen. For some unfortunate kids, that's also a pretty good survival strategy. It's really hard to take a swat at someone who is obviously making an effort to listen to what you're saying. And if that person should take the next step and say back what he or she heard, clearly showing an attempt to understand, then it's difficult not to accord the same respect when it's the other person's turn to speak. Sounds pretty civilized. Teenagers don't always believe me when I tell them that this is powerful stuff. But then they don't have the same confidence as I do in adults' ability to change.

One young man I met recently was very sceptical about this problem-solving approach to dealing with parents. His dad drives him crazy, he said, because whenever he tries to talk about a problem he's dealing with at school, or with friends, or at his part-time job, his father always interrupts with a story about something that happened to him at work. It sounded to me as if Dad was trying to help by finding an analogous situation from his experience that might have relevance for his son, but the kid sure couldn't see the connections and felt that his father wasn't empathizing with him at all. His usual response was to interrupt his father in turn, rage that this wasn't helping, and storm out of the room feeling that Dad had let him down again.

I asked him to imagine for a minute what would happen if he let his father ramble on with his story without interruption and, when he had finished, just say "You have a point, Dad." Not a good point or even a relevant point, but a point. The boy thought about it for a couple of seconds and then started to laugh. His dad would be left speechless. The fact that his son would concede even minimally that he had something to say would change the whole script immediately. The kid couldn't wait to get home and try it.

Learning to negotiate with parents

To me, the vehemence kids put into their stories and the anger they often express aren't such bad things. It's obvious they want their parents to be a resource they can turn to. They need their parents to negotiate with them. The most contempt for a parent I ever heard in the classroom came from an older teenager whose mother wouldn't stand up for herself. Her "Whatever you think, dear" passivity was driving her daughter into a more and more confrontational mode that was putting great stress on the whole family.

I think, at heart, the girl was trying to force her mother to negotiate; when she wouldn't, the daughter's reaction was intense anger. I suspect part of that mother's problem is that she doesn't have the strategies in place that would help her to deal with these issues, so she tries to avoid or withdraw from conflicts. My suggestion to students is that sometimes they need to take the lead in introducing a problem-solving approach into their family interactions, if their parents don't have the knowledge or skills to do it.

I think that sometimes people are unwilling to confront difficult problems because they assume that if, by defining the problem clearly, they discover that they don't agree on the issue, then that's the end to the problem-solving process. They'll just have to agree to disagree. But that doesn't need to be the case. Acknowledging the different perspectives we have on an issue is just the beginning of the negotiation process. From there we can generate alternatives and select the ones that are acceptable from both positions.

We don't need to start from the same point to come, eventually, to a meeting of the minds. However, if we lock into a position and refuse to acknowledge that there's another point of view we won't be able to create the space we need for generating mutually beneficial options. I think that, unconsciously, parents and kids often create opposition by forcing one another into extreme positions.

What if parents don't know how to negotiate?

One girl in a grade nine class showed a good deal of scepticism about finding win-win resolutions to problems that involve parents. I invited her to share an immediate problem with me to see if our problem-solving model could help and she did so, forcefully. She wanted to go a dance being held at her school the next afternoon. It's a school that's had its share of problems, especially at events outside of regular school hours. When she asked her mother's permission, the immediate response was "No way." The inevitable argument ensued.

The girl was surprised when I suggested that she'd forced a confrontation with her mother by the way she raised the issue. Whenever kids ask us a question to which there's an obvious yes or no answer, they're forcing us into taking a position and, being parents, the most natural thing for us to do is take the negative position. Of course we'll say no, given such an easy choice!

I then outlined all the arguments I suspected she had used in trying to get her mother to change her position and the automatic responses I figured her mom had given:

Girl — But all my friends are going.

Mom — What's that got to do with anything? What those other parents choose to do is their business, but you're my daughter and I'm saying no.

Girl — But you never let me do anything. I'm 14 years old and you still treat me like a baby.

Mom	And when you carry on like this, no wonder. There'll be lots of time when you're a bit older to go to all these dances.
Girl	You don't trust me. What did I do to make you not trust me?
Mom	It's not a matter of trust. I've made up my mind and I don't want to discuss it any further.
Girl	You're so mean. I wish you weren't my mother.
Mom	Some day you'll thank me for this. When you have your own children you'll learn it's not so easy being a parent. I remember when I was your age ...

Fill in the rest if you haven't heard enough; you and I both know how it plays out.

I invited the girl to do something really scary for a minute: try to think like her mother. What was the issue for her mother? Why was she so convinced that her decision to deny her daughter permission to attend the dance was the right one? There was silence for quite a while and then the teenager said, "I guess Mom's afraid that something might happen to me at the dance." That's Mom's issue: not fun, not independence, not trust. Safety.

I continued to question her. "So there are the two positions: you want to go to the dance to have fun with your friends; your mom doesn't want you to go because she's concerned about your personal safety. Now we know where you both stand, what could you offer to your mother to address her need to know that you can attend the dance safely?"

Again there was a pause and the daughter suggested, "I could wear a beeper to the dance." That's a good example right there of why parents and kids need to problem-solve together. I don't know what options you would have come up with, but wearing a beeper to a social event isn't something that would spring to my mind — although, interestingly, now that I've heard the suggestion I'm starting to notice lots of ads in magazines and on TV that are promoting security devices for children!

The girl didn't particularly want to wear a beeper to the dance, but that initial idea got us thinking of lots of other ways she could suggest for staying in contact so her mother wouldn't feel negligent in allowing her to attend the dance. And among them all, surely there'd be at least one reasonable solution to put forward.

Notice that by engaging one another in a mutual search for an acceptable solution, we (mother and daughter) are also building commitment to finding some way around the problem that will meet both our needs. We're finding room for negotiation without either of us having to back down, or lose face, or feel that we're not doing what our duty requires. Taking time to explore the problem and generating alternative solutions leads to better problem-solving on both sides.

Finally, we have to be clear about the option we've agreed to try and make sure that we keep up our end of the bargain. If I agree to tell you who I'm going to the dance with and what time I'll be home, and to check in once during the evening by telephone, then I have to follow up on my commitment. If you agree not to give my friends the third degree and to wait for my phone call, not hop in your car and drive by the school just to be sure I made it there safely, then you have to stick to the deal too.

Then tomorrow morning we can sit down together and talk about how it went. Did you enjoy the dance? Could you relax and not check the clock every 15 minutes to see when I would be home? Next time there's a school event and the same kind of question comes up, is there anything we could do differently?

With the daily practice we get in negotiating resolutions to conflicts and making decisions with our kids, we should all be a whole lot smarter and wiser at the end of each day!

Negotiating at school

While many of the natural opportunities for teaching negotiation skills occur at home and on the playground, looking at the academic curriculum with the need to teach this important life skill in mind may also open up some dynamic new approaches to more standard fare.

When I first considered teaching negotiation skills 10 years ago, one of the titles on the course of study for my class was Shakespeare's *The Taming of the Shrew*. I thought it might be interesting to teach the play as showing the process by which a person learns to negotiate. Katherine the Shrew goes from a foul-mouthed, physically abusive young woman to a mature negotiator who understands the context in which she's working and manages to use it to her advantage. Her final speech, which many feminists have shuddered over, can be seen in quite a different light as a woman explaining how women can survive and even thrive in a man's world when they understand the rules of the game.

The Taming of the Shrew is filled with lots of case studies: two sisters renegotiating their relationship, a father and suitor settling the terms of an arranged marriage, a household steward renegotiating working conditions for the help. We considered all of those and then, after we had studied the play and practised our negotiation model, each student had an opportunity to role-play one of those scenarios with me on video. We had already established the criteria for a good negotiation, and now we developed a weighted checklist for assessing the videotaped role-plays.

First the students and I replayed the videos separately and did our individual assessments, and then we came together to negotiate the final grade for their performance. That was the real-life application of our model, when they were no longer characters in an artificial role but true partners in a negotiated assessment process.

What that experience reinforced for me was the belief that academic and social skills can and should be learned together. My students gained a deeper understanding of the play when they could relate the characters' experience to their own lives. At the same time their skill in negotiating was enhanced when they could practise in role, adopting different perspectives and styles from their more natural approach to conflict.

The confidence they showed in negotiating their grades also enhanced the assessment process for both of us. When there was a discrepancy in our evaluation we went to the tape for confirmation. Because they had an opportunity to explain how they felt they had met the criteria for the assignment, they ended up with a much better grasp of the standard they had achieved and where they needed to improve their skills.

Finding the curriculum connections

When I work with classroom teachers who are finding it difficult to see how the teaching of negotiation or other generic skills might be accommodated in their curriculum, my advice is not to range far afield looking for new materials but to look back at the topics and literature they've enjoyed in the past to see how they might be adapted to address this new need.

When I thought about it, I realized that one of the reasons for Shakespeare's ongoing appeal is that his dramas are rooted in human experience. When I work with younger kids I find the stories that appeal most to them are often based on the basic need for kids to learn to get along and negotiate their way in the world.

I'll not soon forget the looks on the faces of some of the parents watching me work with a group of primary kids when we read Paulette Bourgeois' delightful *Franklin Is Bossy*. Franklin the turtle was in danger of being ostracized by his buddies because they were fed up with always having to play the game according to his rules. When I asked the kids if they had any suggestions based on their own experience in dealing with bossy people (older siblings, parents, teachers) they quickly came up with a whole slew of ideas. I showed them a conflict-resolution poster I had brought with me, and they soon realized that in their discussion they had mentioned every idea on that poster, plus a few variations. The parents were surprised by the kids' repertoire of strategies, and we were all reminded of the power of good children's literature in validating kids' experiences.

Using literature is an important strategy, well recognized by the talented developers of several excellent life-skills programs. But teachers of other subject areas don't have to feel left out of the process. I can't think of a single academic area that doesn't have controversial issues students can research in order to develop opposing perspectives as the basis for dialogue and negotiation.

In his CoRT program, De Bono includes a strategy called OPV (other point of view). Using this approach, a teacher might provide students with an article from the newspaper and ask them to summarize the issue as it's presented. They then try to identify from whose perspective the article was written. Using OPV, they brainstorm a list of people who would have a different perspective on the issue and suggest how their opinion might differ from the one presented in the article. Every section of the paper yields possibilities: a sports story about a player trade, a business article about an upcoming merger, a front-page account of a citizen protest, a lost-and-found notice for a missing family pet.

The academic controversy model

Roger and David Johnson have used this idea of helping students to negotiate their way through a complex issue to develop a powerful model they call "academic (or creative) controversy." I recently used it with a group of Family Studies teachers who had expressed concern about the growing number of students who are adopting a vegetarian lifestyle. In the Johnson and Johnson model, students work in pairs to research one side of an issue.

Usually the teacher provides the basic readings, especially when the students are initially being introduced to the controversy process. Together the partners summarize the points they plan to use in support of their argument on the issue. At the same time, another pair of students is using a separate set of materials to develop an opposing argument. When the two pairs are ready, they come together in a group of four to present the two sides of the issue.

In the vegetarian example, the two arguments might go something like this:

Pro: A vegetarian diet is a healthy alternative for teenagers.

- Most teens consume unhealthy levels of junk food, which is high in fat and sodium.
- Following a vegetarian diet forces kids to think about their food choices and makes them more conscious of balancing their diet from the different food groups.
- Obesity rates among teens would go down if they ate more fruits and veggies and pastas.
- Many teens are concerned about the inhumane treatment of domestic animals and are protesting by refusing to eat meat or dairy products.

Con: A vegetarian diet constitutes a health risk for many teenagers.

- Teens are not eating beans, legumes, etc. to replace nutrients lost when they eliminate meat and/or dairy products from their diet.

- Vegetarianism is a fad rather than a conscious nutritional choice.
- Some teens are risking anorexia by not eating enough or by eliminating key elements of a balanced diet.
- There are other effective means for advocating humane treatment of farm animals than boycotting meat products.

Immediately after the first pair present their arguments, their opponents ask questions. The point of the questioning is the key to the Johnson and Johnson model: *understanding and clarifying the other argument, not knocking holes in it.* When the first side is confident that their perspective has been understood, then side two presents the opposing arguments. Again this is followed by questions and clarification.

Why is it so important for the pairs to be clear about what they've heard? Because the next step is to reverse perspectives. In fact, when they present their new case they try to do a better job than their opponents did in the first place! They add supporting facts where they can and use all their skills of persuasion to defend the new point of view.

The final step is for the four group members to put their heads together to write a joint report that summarizes the best points from both arguments. Having looked at the issue from both perspectives, they try to reach a consensus based on their shared understanding of the facts and their interpretation of the significance of those facts. If the report includes points the group feels aren't conclusive, the need for further information may lead to some group investigation and further reporting.

The built-in opportunities for developing negotiation skills are an obvious advantage of this approach. However, there are other benefits as well. Controversial issues are often the first things to be eliminated when textbooks go through the editing and validation processes, and yet what is cutting edge in a field is often what gets students really excited about learning. When they begin to realize that every area of knowledge has more to it than the dusty facts found in a reference book, they may also begin to think of themselves as people who have something to contribute to that body of knowledge, rather than passive receptacles for regurgitated information.

The benefit from a teacher's perspective is that something weird happens as kids work through the steps in the process. I may have started out with very little interest in vegetarianism, but by the time I've finished presenting both sides of the argument my interest has probably quickened. The brain's a strange thing: what it thinks about it usually ends up liking. As with people, time spent in the company of new ideas often leads to new friendships.

SUMMARY

Making decisions is one form of problem-solving, negotiating another, and to become successful in the "real world" children need to learn how to do both. Another important real-life skill that we need to model in our relationships with children is being able to understand and respond to different perspectives.

CHAPTER 11

SMART KIDS

In the collection of his writings called *The School as a Home for the Mind*, Art Costa has a wonderful chapter called "The search for intelligent life" in which he outlines 14 traits, or behaviours, that are common among smart people. At the end of a summer school session I taught recently I used a chart developed from Costa's book to have my students think about their own behaviours. For each trait listed on the chart I asked them to identify something they had done during the previous month — in the classroom, at home, or in another context — that was evidence of that type of behaviour.

I'd like to use a similar approach in this concluding chapter, not only to review the kinds of thoughtful behaviours we hope to instil in kids, but also to think about the characteristics of homes and schools that support the kids' social and intellectual development. Costa uses an interesting word to capture this combination of behaviours. He calls it *efficacy*: confidence that through the application of our best thinking we can make a difference in our own lives and the lives of those we touch.

Here's a quick catalogue of Costa's 14 traits:

- persistence;
- decreased impulsiveness;
- listening to others with understanding and empathy;
- social intelligence;
- flexibility;
- metacognition;
- accuracy and precision;
- a sense of humour;
- questioning and problem-posing;
- transferring prior learning to new situations;
- risk-taking;
- using all the senses;
- creativity;
- inquisitiveness and wonder.

A lot of recent media attention has been devoted to a book by Dan Goleman called *Emotional Intelligence*. Goleman explains why qualities like persistence, empathy and the ability to control impulsiveness are the key to success in school, work and personal relationships. But what delighted me most about his book was a discussion in the final chapter of how home and school can work together to help kids of all ages to develop these qualities. He's very clear about the need to incorporate *emotional literacy* into the daily life of the classroom and draws a direct parallel between school and home:

> "... like good childrearing at home, the lessons imparted are small but telling, delivered regularly and over a sustained period of years. That is how emotional learning becomes ingrained; as experiences are repeated over and over, the brain reflects them as strengthened pathways, neural habits to apply in times of duress, frustration, hurt." (p.263)

Goleman also reminds us of the important modelling that teachers and other adults provide:

> "Whenever a teacher responds to one student, twenty or thirty others learn a lesson." (p.279)

Costa talks about this too, with a concept he calls *vertical continuity*. Whatever behaviours we have in mind for children must be an integral part of the daily interactions they have with adults. Costa is specific that those models must reach from the bottom to the top of current educational hierarchies:

> "If we wish to install intelligent behaviour as a significant outcome of education, the instructional strategies, purposefully intended to develop children's metacognitive abilities, must be infused into our teaching methods, staff development, and supervisory processes." (p.88)

I hope you agree that we have to add parenting processes to that list as well.

What's happening in the schools?

If current research by behavioural scientists isn't enough, reports on school effectiveness might be more convincing. They also stress the need to pay attention to intelligence in all its forms. Two years ago the *Toronto Star* ran an interesting back-to-school article with an attention-catching headline: *Three Rs not so vital at top schools: report* (Friday, August 25, 1995). A 2.5 million dollar national study of exemplary Canadian secondary schools found that those schools went far beyond traditional academics in order to consider "the moral and social parts of schooling." Their goals were to teach students to be mature, critical, moral thinkers. In addressing these goals, they naturally formed partnerships with parents, businesses and community agencies in order to create a better learning environment for all students, including those at risk of dropping out.

Over the last year I had an opportunity to work with a school that I think meets a number of the criteria included in that government report. It's a small alternative secondary school that draws students from across our system. Its program was originally designed for adolescents who were self-directed in their learning: kids who would enjoy an informal atmosphere with fewer structured classes and more opportunities for independent research or small-group seminars.

Many of the students thrived in that setting; for example, the school had a small team of university-bound students with an established reputation as champion debaters. But over the years the profile of the student body changed as a number of students (and some referring high schools) began to see the program as an escape for kids who were having difficulty fitting into or meeting the academic expectations of more traditional schools. Those students weren't always prepared to or willing to take on more responsibility for their own learning. So this school, which began with a fairly homogeneous student body and a clear mission, was now experiencing the diversity of student needs and the multiple agendas that are the norm in most urban schools.

What to do? One possibility was to go back to the basics. (That always seems to come up as an option when schools are going through transitional pains these days!) In this case that would mean more screening of potential students to try to identify those the program was originally designed to serve. But the staff was open to other suggestions.

I had earlier attended a session on problem-based learning, a curriculum model originally used in training medical students but now being adapted for use in elementary and secondary schools. It's an incredibly exciting innovation that brings together many of the themes explored in this book: opportunities for building thinking into daily practice, collaboration with students in designing curriculum, new roles for teachers, partnerships with experts in the community, etc. I thought it might provide the new focus that alternative school was looking for, while also appealing to a wider range of students.

The response from the staff is a good example to me of what Costa was describing. They didn't rush to make any decisions; they agreed to give themselves a year to explore this option. That meant doing a lot of background reading and talking among themselves. They also prepared a funding proposal that allowed them to access staff development funds from several sources and, with that money, they arranged a three-day training session for their staff and the three members of my centrally assigned office. As a group, we went through the learning process that was being considered for the students.

The staff also invited a number of their students to meet the trainer and practise the model with some of the teachers, so they could get a feel for what it might be like to work in this investigative model. Staff members began discussions with parents to get their input about the proposed project. Whether their final decision is to adopt the problem-based learning model for their school or not, the experience for the staff has been illuminating.

In small pockets of innovation, this is what reflective practitioners are doing all across North America. Whether the proposed changes are designed to implement research on brain-based learning, co-operative learning, education for social responsibility, the inclusion of special-needs students in regular classrooms, early or later literacy programs, new standards in mathematics or technology, authentic assessment, transition to employment, constructivism — you name it, the maxim holds true. Whatever we want for or from our kids, they are most likely to do as we do.

From school to home

In our school board, significant changes have been made to report cards in the last few years. The front still gives information about the student's progress and achievement in literacy, numeracy and individual subject areas. But it's the back that interests me. It shows a movement away from generalized comments in the non-academic areas to specific assessment that tracks progress over time. Included there, as well as a section for the assessment of the development of personal and social responsibility, is a section for the assessment of cross-curricular outcomes related to thinking skills, information management and study habits. There's also a place for the student to reflect on his or her progress and set personal goals.

The initial feedback I've heard from teachers is that they're having a hard time with the back sections. Why? Because it's almost impossible to complete them without input from other teachers, from the parents and from the children themselves. They focus exactly on the question behind what I've been saying in this book: have our students got the skills they need not only to do well in the academic areas traditionally assessed but also to progress toward the goal of lifelong learning in the world beyond the classroom?

That's a complex question. But my hope is that, as teachers are confronted more and more frequently with questions of this sort, the two needs I've stressed — the need to teach transferable thinking skills and the need to establish a partnership between home and school — will come increasingly to the fore in their thoughts and plans.

Ways we can support intelligent behaviour

Like the students in my summer class, let's think about what we might offer as evidence, as teachers and parents, that we are providing smart schools and smart homes. Here's a beginning list:

Behaviour	Classroom	Home
Persistence	Encourage students to revisit prior learning to see how time and effort have paid off.	Support your children's multiple attempts at new learning tasks.

Impulse control	Teach anger management techniques like counting backwards and deep breathing.	Use time out instead of physical discipline.
Empathetic listening	Wait to be sure students are finished speaking before responding.	Paraphrase to be sure you've understood your child's intent.
Sociability	Teach pro-social skills and structure regular co-operative learning activities.	Coach the children in new social situations.
Flexible thinking	Pose open-ended questions.	Consider your child's perspective when solving family problems.
Metacognition	Keep a teaching journal; join a staff study group.	Spend five minutes in conversation with each child daily.
Accuracy/ precision	Provide models of craftsmanship so students know what good work looks like.	Build a vocabulary of feeling so your children can express their emotions clearly.
Humour	Wear your green hat and cut loose on occasion.	Never tell your kids "Don't be silly!"
Questioning/ problem-posing	Structure lessons around the students' questions.	"Did you ask a good question today, Izzy?"
Transferring	Welcome the question "Why do we have to learn this?" (If the kids forget to ask, do it yourself.)	Ask teachers to suggest ways to reinforce learning at home.

Risk-taking	Defer evaluation so the students have time to make mistakes.	Help the children identify what they learned in failing that will help them next time.
Using all senses	Use Gardner's eight intelligences in designing instruction.	Support arts education as essential to educating the whole child.
Creativity	Never allow external rewards to undermine the joy of self-expression.	Talk about what things could be rather than what they are. Start a lot of sentences with "What if ...?"
Curiosity/ wonder	Make time for students to investigate their own interests. Expand the walls of the classroom.	Know what fascinates your children and feed their curiosity. Let them teach you something new.

Can you add to my list? I'm sure you will as you discover your own strategies for promoting intelligence in the classroom and at home.

SUMMARY

If intelligent behaviour is to become a significant outcome of education, parents and teachers must work together to help children develop the specific qualities that characterize smart people. By honing our thinking skills, we can make a difference in our own lives and the lives of others.

CONCLUSION

I've shared a lot of personal anecdotes throughout this book, so I guess it's fitting that I close with one last story. For a number of years I taught an elective course to students in their final year of high school. Invariably, sometime during the year I would recite one of my favourite quotations from literature, which exhorts each of us to search for new challenges and not be afraid to risk failure. Solemnly, feelingly I would intone: "A man's reach should exceed his grasp or what's a heaven for?" Being a good English teacher, I'd credit my source: Alexander Pope in his "Essay on Man."

Occasionally one of the keener students would follow up on that little gem and go to Pope's poem to see what else he had to say. Several of them came back to announce they were having trouble finding those exact words. Was I maybe misquoting? No, no I would assure them. I'd taken several courses in which Pope's "Essay" was required reading. It's a long poem; they must have overlooked those lines. But over the years a niggling suspicion began to develop that maybe it was something else Pope wrote. I began citing the author but leaving out the title of the poem.

A few years ago, when I was reorganizing my bookshelves, I found the textbook we'd used in grade 13. Flipping through it, I came upon the poem "Andrea del sarto" by Robert Browning. And there in plain type were the words: "A man's reach should ..." Mortification. All those years of pontificating about the glory of setting uplifting if unattainable goals for oneself and I couldn't even get the author right!

However, practising what I've learned in the interim, I'm being metacognitive about my little mistake. Just think how intently my students read Pope's poem over the years, trying to find a quotation that wasn't there. If I'd got it right, they probably would have found it instantly, crossed it off and gone on to the next. In retrospect, my error was probably a good thing.

Who says teachers are infallible anyway?

BIBLIOGRAPHY

If *Smart Homes + Smart Schools = Smart Kids* has aroused your curiosity about the newest ideas in teaching thinking, please note that, in addition to the books referred to in the text, this bibliography includes several titles that interested parents and teachers will find both readable and enlightening. For each group, I've chosen 10 titles I feel may be of special interest. These are marked in the bibliography as follows:

★ = Top 10 choices for parents
✔ = Top 10 choices for teachers

Happy reading!

★ ASCD. *What's New in School?* (Video series) Association for Supervision and Curriculum Development, 1996.

Barell, John. *Teaching for Thoughtfulness.* Longman, 1991.

Bourgeois, Paulette. *Franklin Is Bossy.* Kids Can Press, 1993.

Bruner, Jerome. Quoted from *The Process of Education* in Peter B. Dow, *Schoolhouse Politics.* Harvard University Press, 1991.

Buzan, Tony. *Use Both Sides of Your Brain.* 3rd ed. E.P. Dutton, 1989.

✔ Caine, Geoffrey, Renate Nummela Caine and Sam Crowell. *Mindshifts: A Brain-Based Process for Restructuring Schools and Renewing Education.* Zephyr Press, 1994.

Carmody, Bruce. Principal's message in William G. Miller Junior Public School Newsletter. February, 1991.

Cohen, Miriam. *First Grade Takes a Test.* Dell, 1980.

★ Coloroso, Barbara. *Kids Are Worth It.* William Morrow and Co., 1994.

Costa, Art. "Re-assessing Assessment" in *Educational Leadership.* Vol. 46, No. 7, April 1989, 2.

Costa, Art. *The School as a Home for the Mind.* IRI Skylight, 1991.

✔ Costa, Art and Robert Garmston. *Cognitive Coaching: A Foundation for Renaissance Schools.* Christopher-Gordon Publishers Inc., 1994.

★ Covey, Stephen. *The 7 Habits of Highly Effective People.* Simon and Schuster, 1989.

✔ Davidson, Neil and Toni Worsham, eds. *Enhancing Thinking Through Cooperative Learning.* Teachers College Press, 1992.

De Bono, Edward. *The CoRT Thinking Program.* Pergamon Press, 1987.

★ De Bono, Edward. *Six Thinking Hats.* Penguin, 1995.

✔ De Bono, Edward. *Six Thinking Hats for Schools.* (Four resource books, K-12) Perfection Learning, 1991.

Dillon, James Thomas. *Questioning and Teaching: A Manual of Practice.* Teachers College Press, 1988.

Duckworth, Eleanor. *"The Having of Wonderful Ideas" and Other Essays on Teaching and Learning.* Teachers College Press, 1987.

Dunn, R. and K. Dunn. *Teaching Students Through Their Individual Learning Styles.* Prentice-Hall, Inc., 1978.

★ Faber, Adele and Elaine Mazlish. *How to Talk So Kids Can Learn at Home and in School.* Simon and Schuster, 1995.

★ Faber, Adele and *How to Talk So Kids Will Listen and Listen So Kids Will Talk.* Avon Books, 1980.

Fulghum, Robert. "A Bag of Possibles and Other Matters of the Mind" in *Newsweek Special Issue.* Fall/Winter 1990, 88-92.

★ ✔ Gardner, Howard. *The Unschooled Mind: How Children Think and How Schools Should Teach.* Basic Books, 1991.

Generic Skills/Economic Development. Final Report Pilot Phase. March 6, 1987. H.H. Russell, Principle Investigator. Research funded by Ministry of Education, Ministry of Colleges and Universities, Ministry of Skills Development, Ministry of Labour, Ontario.

Gibbs, Jeanne. *Tribes: A New Way of Learning and Being Together.* Centre Source Systems, 1995.

★ ✔ Goleman, Daniel. *Emotional Intelligence.* Bantam Books, 1995.

Howe, James. *Bunnicula.* Avon Books, 1978.

✔ Hyerle, David. *Visual Tools for Constructing Knowledge.* ASCD, 1996.

Johnson, David W. and Roger T. Johnson. *Creative Controversy: Intellectual Challenge in the Classroom.* Interaction Book Co., 1992.

Kingsley, Daniel T. *How to Fire an Employee.* Facts on File Publications, 1984.

Kletzien, Sharon and Barbara Conway Hushion. "Reading Workshop: Reading, Writing, Thinking" in *Journal of Reading.* 35 (6), 444-451.

Kohn, Alfie. *Punished by Rewards: The Trouble with Gold stars, Incentive Plans, A's, Praise, and Other Bribes.* Houghton Mifflin, 1993.

Langer, Ellen. *Mindfulness.* Addison-Wesley, 1989.

Lions-Quest. *Skills for Action.* Quest International, 1995.

Lowry, Don. *True Colors®:The Show.* Communication Companies International, 1989.

Margulies, Nancy. *Mapping Inner Space.* Zephyr Press, 1991.

McCarthy, Bernice et al. *The 4Mat System: Teaching to Learning Styles with Right/Left Mode Techniques.* Excel, 1980.

Myers, Isabel Briggs. *Introduction to Type: A Description of the Theory and Application of the Myers-Briggs Type Indicator.* Consulting Psychologists Press, Inc., 1987.

Parks, Sandra and Howard Black. *Organizing Thinking. Book 1.* Critical Thinking Press and Software, 1992.

✔ Perkins, David. *Outsmarting I.Q.: The Emerging Science of Learnable Intelligence.* Free Press, 1995.

Perkins, David. *Smart Schools: From Training Memories to Educating Minds.* Free Press, 1992.

Perkins, David and G. Saloman. "Teaching for Transfer" in *Educational Leadership.* 46 (1), 22-32.

★ Rich, Dorothy. *MegaSkills: How Families Can Help Children Succeed in School and Beyond.* Houghton Mifflin, 1988.

Sternberg, Robert. "Answering Questions and Questioning Answers" in *Phi Delta Kappan.* 76 (2), 136-138.

★ ✔ Sternberg, Robert. *Successful Intelligence: How Practical and Creative Intelligence Determine Success in Life.* Simon and Schuster, 1996.

Sternberg, Robert. *The Triarchic Mind: A New Theory of Human Intelligence.* Viking, 1988.

Sternberg, Robert and John Kolligan Jr., eds. *Competence Considered.* Yale University Press, 1990.

Sternberg, Robert and Richard Wagner, eds. *Mind in Context.* Cambridge University Press, 1994.

Stiggins, Richard. "Assessment Literacy" in *Phi Delta Kappan.* 72 (7), 534-539.

Swartz, Robert and Sandra Parks. *Infusing the Teaching of Critical and Creative Thinking into Content Instruction.* Critical Thinking Press and Software, 1994.

Timpe, A. Dale. *Motivation of Personnel.* Facts on File Publications, 1986.

✔ Udall, Anne and Joan Daniels. *Creating the Thoughtful Classroom.* Zephyr Press, 1991.

What Work Requires of Schools: A SCANS Report for America 2000. The Secretary's Commission on Achieving Necessary Skills, 1991.

Wiederhold, Charles. *Cooperative Learning and Critical Thinking: The Question Matrix.* Resources for Teachers, Inc., 1990.

Wycoff, Joyce. *Mindmapping: Your Personal Guide to Exploring Creativity and Problem-Solving.* Berkley Books, 1991.